Life In The Diaspora:

Adventure across four continents

By

Hillary Rono

December 2017

Life in The Diaspora:

Adventure Across Four Continents

Contents

Dedication

The book *Life in The Diaspora* examines a self-made journey in The Diaspora across four continents: Africa, America, Europe, and Asia and the Middle East. It was a pain-staking journey that required highly select virtues in life, high discipline with continuous improvement, the ability to make fast decisions, being in the right place at the right time, and, most importantly unwavering belief in God.

To my mum, Rael Chebunyei, and late dad, Samuel Tigirer Chebunyei, I say you taught us the importance of observing law, respecting others, and learning the blessings of being a giver rather than a receiver. Much appreciation to my lovely wife, Dorcas Rono, and my boys, Dylan, Nathaniel, and Finley, for the great support you have given me while I wrote this book miles away from England, our new home. I dedicate this book to my best friend and wife, Dorcas, a selfless icon, a person coincidentally the same as the Dorcas of the Bible. Dedication too to mum-in-law Jane Koskey: your great example of hospitality does shine in The Diaspora. Indeed, I wrote the book 3,702 miles far away from family in England but perhaps it was time well spent away from family; it involved many hours of exciting late-night weekend writing in the middle of an extremely busy and great job which required equal attention.

To my brothers and sisters in Africa and in some parts of the world, I may not mention you by name due to the focused context of this book, but we have supported each other and succeeded well in life.

To my esteemed readers, I hope you find this book inspiring, contending, and fulfilling, and a useful guide in your endeavours in The Diaspora.

To the nations of the world and people therein, The Diaspora has built the world right from the ancient times and more dramatically after the Second World War. The Diaspora ought to be continuously respected and protected, since a diverse world is what we strive for, and we see this coming together and breaking of walls of isolations during key international tournaments such as the Olympics and the World Cups.

Foreword

Being far from the comforts of home and comfort zone has informed writing this book with the hope that those in The Diaspora will benefit immensely.

I, Hillary Rono, a fifth-born child in a family of eleven, am clearly the median child in a large and extended family in Africa. I found success or failure in life to be a product of the ability to tackle and balance life challenges and opportunities, to believe in the fact that it being better to try and fail rather than not try at all, and to walk the talk by doing things and having the will and energy to act. Born in Cheborge village, Bureti District, Kenya, my parents moved to Rongai, Nakuru, Kenya, in 1977 when I was just two years old. Obviously it is hard for anyone to remember how life was at two, but my life in The Diaspora started at the age of two and continues to date nearly four decades later, and affirms the fact that The Diaspora is an inevitable part of life.

I spent nine continuous years as an adult in one Diaspora country in the West, a country that is considered one of the great empires in the modern world, the UK. The nine continuous years spent as an adult in one of The Diaspora country is equal in length to a full life in a primary school, and therefore provides an opportunity for extraordinary reflections on The Diaspora in the modern times. Having spent earlier life in rural Kenya and later life in The Diaspora really means that I can claim to provide a meaningful contrast of life in two different settings and shed some light on what constitutes success in The Diaspora.

Quite often, especially in previously colonised countries, I have met people in life who have challenged my stay in The Diaspora and expressly said that I could be much better off, perhaps more rich, in Africa than in The West. In the past there was some talk of slavery in the West and the need to shun countries that enslaved Africa, but Nelson Mandela had a formidable and successful counter-narrative to this. I have heard plenty of narrative about the failure of the West, double standards, hypocrisy, and other counter-narratives. Sometimes others told me "go adventure in The West but don't stay too long out there, don't return as a pensioner". I must admit, this has been confusing and it has taken me time to define what matters to me in life, free from easy and cheap generality. Is it riches, comfort, justice, wealth, knowledge, technology, or put simply and generically: is it materialism or other intangible or crucial and more important pressing issues in life that really matter? The answer is complicated and professors in business school in America where I studied MBA told us a "yes or no" answer is not good enough with the best answer being "it depends".

My family in Africa was and remains quite large and I am extremely proud of this. My family is larger than any other average African family but perhaps not so big like the Solomon Empire in the biblical time, though we have diverse talents in the larger family which form a formidable force to reckon with. In the African context, a large African family was a deterrent against external aggression. To put it simply, a large family was a "nuclear" deterrent of ancient life. In those days, a larger family in Africa operated like modern NATO in terms of safety and security, and we considered messing with one member of a large family as an insult to the wider clan which would attract firm, swift, and severe action, similar to the shock and awe of American self-determination after September 11th. This

6

principle enabled large African families to survive multiple environments, circumstances, and often situations and terrains. And to me, family remains indispensable and I would not even listen to anyone or any institution lecture me on how to bring up a modern family that treasures the simple basics of yesterday's years which kept families going extremely well, long before powerful governments and too many laws existed. Even before I knew what government is all about, my parents in rural Africa had already taught me the basics in life and with all due respect, I still believe modern nations are stronger when families are stronger.

Unfortunately, modernity is shunning the role of the family at an alarming rate. In the modern world, having a family is no longer as fashionable as it used to be because of endless excitements that are perceived as necessary to be enjoyed before one starts a family. But unless the world returns to the basics that held families solid for so long, the future without stable families is worrying. Many people left or still leave for The Diaspora as single individuals but the family established in The Diaspora helped shape the future, including that of The Diaspora driven nations.

The Diaspora in modern times

The Diaspora in the modern time is very different from The Diaspora in ancient times because we live in a virtually claimed Earth, one hundred per cent owned, where at least somebody owns somewhere and everywhere; the land mass on Earth is claimed while international waters, mainly sea, is already demarcated either to individual nations or owned collectively by nations of the world, with clear rules of engagements.

To readers of this book and perhaps for many people around the world, modern The Diaspora life starts or may be deemed to start the moment one boards a plane or other international vessel of travel, to travel to the far distant world, to the unknown which quite often looks like or is made to look like the land of Canaan, with plenty of milk and honey even long before arrival. I have been lucky to spend most of my time in The Diaspora, so The Diaspora has been part and parcel of my life. My first job after university was in The Diaspora, a job in Hargeisa, Somaliland, with an international NGO based in Nairobi, Kenya. It is quite interesting that my first country in The Diaspora, the Somaliland, has been refused international recognition, which is quite understandable in a way since no country, however powerful, would like to mess with the status quo, more so touching on national sovereignty and boundaries. To date, I am still in The Diaspora, some four thousand miles from my new home of England and seven hundred miles from my home of birth in Kenya.

People head to The Diaspora for many reasons but the widely known reasons are economic, educational, social, or for security. A declining or bad economy drives people away from areas of economic unrest and turmoil into stable economies with hope, promise, rule of law, and better prospects for the future. Many still go to The Diaspora in search of higher education in advanced economies. Sometimes migration to The Diaspora could be for social reasons, especially to join those who left in advance, like those who left to unclaimed lands in advance in decades past. Conflicts around the world have always created insecurity which drives large masses of populations from their homeland into The Diaspora, and the Syrian case is a perfect and modern example.

Survival in The Diaspora is never easy and those who have passed through hardships are normally best placed to survive in a new environment. If one is lucky to endure hardships—which as we have seen in the recent past involves even younger children going through the unbelievable, sometimes stormy seas and oceans—the international community must act quickly to deploy the best of international diplomacy to solve modern and complicated conflicts and the widely ignored, The Diaspora, may have good solutions as they have tasted both life from exile and in sanctuary.

At the national level, rural-to-urban migration is already considered as migration to The Diaspora. I grew up in Kenya and have seen members of nearly every family in Kenya migrate from rural to urban areas in search of better opportunities. Therefore this book not only helps The Diaspora nationally, but The Diaspora in international settings as well.

The Diaspora in ancient times

It is fascinating how the Earth was subdivided into nations with accelerated founding of many nations especially after the end of the British Empire. Quite often, the founders of new nations were The Diaspora, courageous people themselves escaping troubles from home. The account in Genesis 11 describes how man had wanted to build a tower that reached the heavens, but God intervened and thwarted the plan to build a tower and instead scattered the once united people with one language, thus fulfilling God's desire for mankind to disperse and occupy the entire Earth. Sometimes I wonder whether this God's event is responsible for the many languages in The Diaspora right from the ancient times.

God has quite often used The Diaspora to achieve big missions. God asked Abraham to leave his comfort zone into a land he was shown. Joseph left his family and proceeded into The Diaspora and became very prominent in Egypt. Moses too, also a member of The Diaspora, delivered Israelites from bondage.

In the New Testament Bible, scholars have argued that The Diaspora is mentioned several times with some of the noticeable ones being namely: John 7:35, James 1:1, and Peter 1:1.

- John 7:35 – "Then the Jews said among themselves, "Where does He intend to go that we shall not find him? Does He intend to go to the Dispersion among the Greeks and teach the Greeks?"

- James 1:1 – "James, a bond servant of God and of the Lord Jesus Christ, To the twelve tribes which are scattered abroad"
- Peter 1:1 – "Peter, an apostle of Jesus Christ, To the pilgrims of the Dispersion in Pontus, Galatia, Cappadocia, Asia and Bithynia,"

The three books above all contain the words "disperse" or "scatter". Even in ancient times, The Diaspora still existed, and John 7:35 clearly shows that The Diaspora was a far distant land then because modern means of travel were yet to be invented. Clearly, experience in The Diaspora of modern times is a far better adventure compared to The Diaspora in ancient times.

Mass migration of people in ancient times led to The Diaspora. Migration was either forced or occurred naturally as a result of human aspiration to seek a better life away from familiar places into far distant lands. The Assyrian, Babylonian, and Roman Empires forced native people from their homelands. In the bible books of John and James, the Israelites were scattered, while in the book of Peter, God's elect scattered mainly on mission work to spread the word of God.

For the Israelites, The Diaspora, the Bible speaks about God returning them to their homeland from The Diaspora. In 14 May 1948, Israel was again founded as a nation in an instant proclamation, thus fulfilling the prophecy in Isaiah 66:7–8.

What matters in The Diaspora, especially in ancient times, is playing by the rules and laws, hard work, and discipline. The three key factors still matter today.

11

Rules and laws

Many people quite often get to learn about rules, which are generally accepted regulations that govern how to do things as well as a code of conduct in a society. At a tender age, rules are learnt slowly and one by one in a progression but starting from the basics, so as to build the strongest foundation possible. If there is something very fundamental in The Diaspora it is the importance of observing rules in a host country. Observing the law and rule of law is the most important discipline in The Diaspora. Many people get into trouble in The Diaspora just for flouting rules, known or unknown, and we know ignorance of the law is not a defence. Some of the basic rules we learn from young ages, that is to say five years before starting primary school, play a very important role later in life.

The words "rules" and "law" can be used interchangeably. When people speak and talk about rules, it can actually mean written law. But even apart from written law, there are rules that exist in every society and aim to promote social cohesion.

Hard work and discipline

Being in The Diaspora requires hard work and discipline. In an environment known to have a cut-off for success, it is only hard work and discipline that guarantees one to be above the cut-off. In high school, where it was only top colleagues per class and in the whole stream that made it to the public universities, hard work and discipline was the only hope for success, to remain at the top and thus manage to get a space in very competitive public universities. Hard work and discipline must be consistently practiced to show good results in the long haul. To consistently work hard requires good planning which supports the overall objective.

If hard work, discipline, consistency, and good planning are pursued then success is almost guaranteed. This strategy worked for me in both primary and secondary school and I was able to secure a place in a very competitive public university.

Competition and strategy

Even though hard work and discipline may guarantee success, it is always important for one to consider competition. Competitive environments require one to double or triple hard work and discipline. In a competitive environment, strategy matters a lot.

The first time I saw strategy work was when I was in high school. At that time, the school was able to secure a place for around eighty to one hundred students in public university. So in five streams of two hundred students (or forty per class) only eighty to one hundred made it to public university per year, therefore I knew I needed to be at least in position fifteen in my class of forty as a worst case scenario. In four years of high school, the plan was to aim at position fifteen in a class, then work progressively to the top. By third year, the plan was to be among the top five in class. It has been too long since then to remember the exact ranking but I was always top twenty in a stream of two hundred students. I cannot say I was brighter than other students because the school admitted students who had nearly equal marks from primary school so the entry point was same. Subsequent success depended on the strategy one used as well as hard work and discipline. **The strategy is captured in Slide 1 below.**

It was indeed great fun to see a strategy work out successfully, a strategy that I would use throughout my life to date. In a competitive environment, strategy is the gateway to success and helps avoid poor performance. Successful strategy must be well thought out, planned, flexible, emergent at times, and dynamic so as to fit with ever-changing circumstances. My first strategy in high school was successful and this gave me a craving for self-determination in my subsequent pursuits.

After my high school strategy worked, I knew I had secured admission to public university. A grade of B was guaranteed as a minimum. My next strategy was to plan what to do whilst I waited for admission to public university. My parents were farmers and small business entrepreneurs so gaining admission to public university was big achievement since I did not need to worry about huge investment, especially financially, in private university which has been known to sometimes make parents financially worse off, since return on investment may not be very quick.

While waiting to join university I thought of middle level college. I had many options to think through, which included accountancy, agricultural, teaching or education, law or business courses. By using the **criteria of elimination**, I started the process of making a choice; **in Slide 2 below** you will find the three important stages in a career choice. Law was ruled out since to study law in Kenya, one needed an average score of grade A and I knew this was impossible by then. I was not so good at English as I disliked theoretical study of English, so I had ruled out teaching or education even though I was passionate about business and accountancy—so teaching was ruled out. I found agriculture to be good, however, since I was brought up in the countryside I really wanted to get out of my comfort zone. I really wanted to move out of the country life into the city and finally, I opted to pursue accountancy. By then, qualifying as an accountant was a license to better and bigger things. The world-famous Certified Public Accountant, the three letters CPA with a "K" at the end for "Kenya", was just too posh to ignore. It was a guarantee to a good life including the best-looking girls one could ever come across.

Slide 2 - The three Important Stages in Career Choice
by Hillary Rono @ Life in The Diaspora

First, have a pool of career choices, then build a strong case for a specific choice, then make the decision. Stick and live by it. But *always leave options open* hence the flat top

Decision: Accounting

Build strong case for career choice: personal interest, finances, time and future

Career Choice: Accounting (such as CPA, ACCA, CIMA), agriculture, teaching or education, law or business courses

15

I hailed from the countryside and I knew studying in the city was a nightmare in terms of cost. Interestingly, I never wanted to bother my parents since I knew they had imminent university education to sponsor me with. I had an elder brother in the city Nairobi and since I came from large family I knew for sure that I needed to start from somewhere. I therefore convinced my mum to ask my elder brother if I could stay in his place so as to study accountancy while I waited to start university. My brother was very kind, extremely kind, and he never hesitated and told my mum that it was alright for me to relocate to the city, even right away if I was prepared. I was extremely pleased and prepared in the July of 1994 to join my brother in Nairobi to start my CPA studies.

My life in the city had been prepared in advance by a number of factors, perhaps known to me only as I never shared with anyone as naturally I am a very covert person especially where critical. One of the most important aspects was the employment situation. Back in the countryside, I knew several business executives heading key government institutions. There is one executive my dad was so close to; in fact, my dad used to provide him with transport services when we were young. Something happened which taught me great lessons early in life, and such experiences have inspired me to write this book as a dedication to any person hustling the hard way in life. Just after high school, in November 1993, I was keen to get a job and had already drafted my CV (or resume as they call it in the United States). I managed to personally secure an appointment with the executive who would normally spend weekends at his countryside farm, and on weekends apparently includes the best English breakfast in that Kenyan village, just a few miles from my Parents in rural Kenya.

It took me three appointments to see him, and in those two appointments I gave up after securing appointments only to wait in his house from 8 a.m. to 12 p.m. when apparently he would wake up for a full English breakfast in rural Kenya. I was extremely patient and waited until it was just too much to wait any longer. On the third attempt, I managed to see him and I had less than five minutes to say what I wanted. I went straight to the point and introduced myself in the name of my father, the famous and hardworking farmer and small business entrepreneur hustling successfully in life. The chief executive recognised me and he took my CV which he promised to review and update me in due course—that was around January 1994.

I waited for days, weeks, and on the second month I was approached by the gardener of the chief executive who asked me, "Hillary, did you give out your CV to the chief executive?." Well, I was thrilled, hoping to hear the good news. As you can imagine, what else would excite a fresh man from high school than a job to earn a living and pay his fair share in the world and help family who had sacrificed all they had to give me education against all odds? The short-lived news soon became bad news. The gardener told me, "Hillary, don't be shocked, but to tell you the truth, I found your CV in the dustbin while empting the trash bins of my boss, the chief executive." It was indeed painful and I saw at a young age the difficulties of making it in life in Kenya. To me, this was a reminder about all the bad things that could happen in life: rejection, nepotism, favouritism, tribalism and other forms of discrimination and vices that violate equal opportunities, a progressive model in the model world that every country must adopt. I was not disappointed by not getting the job, but by being told my CV was in the dustbin; it would have been better if he gave me proper advice as an experienced chief executive.

While newly arrived in the city of Nairobi from rural Kenya, the incident about "my CV in the bin" shaped my life by then and to date, to an extend that I will not trade any form of discrimination for equal opportunity. While staying in my brother's house I was lucky in the sense that I got all I needed including daily editions of two national newspapers, namely The Daily Nation and The Standard newspapers. I made the two newspapers my *constant companion*, my darlings, especially the one for Wednesday and Friday as it listed plenty of competitive jobs. I was a freshman from high school in a beautiful city with great climate (of no summer and no winter) and could not really qualify for most of the jobs but I remained exceptionally positive I would get something; I can remember vaguely but I may have even applied for CEO positions, out of the determination to get somewhere and pay for my fair share in life. I started the search for employment and because I treasured my education, I never got tempted to do odd jobs to survive since my brother was there, a very generous person who was more fatherly than even a big brother. If there is something I blame my brother for, it was five-star food and a very nice self-contained bedroom that could have tempted me to sleep more and read less.

The good food would later make my life miserable after I left his place, since I did not know how to cook; while the self-contained room with, amazingly, the best bed I had ever slept in by that age, and would quite often make me get tempted to sleep instead of reading hard. It was not easy leaving the bed early in the mornings to study but thankfully I had strong resolve to succeed, hardened by the extraordinary exposure to our society in Kenya.

My search for employment was very bumpy and turbulent, like life itself. But I do not give up easily and nobody should. Job applications by then were exclusively via post office submission, a boring means that was a terrible contrast to modernity, and one had to affix stamps to an envelope, the stamps that could be annoying when it failed to work. In the three months I was with my elder brother, I had made over 200 job applications with not a single post high school certificate in my hand. I applied for jobs with the hope and pledge to attain at least one post high school certificate in the near future; my aim was to work while I studied for a course, which was accountancy (CPA), and hoped employers would share in my vision. One of the job applications, which I had no certificate to back it up except my high school grades and amazing "school leaving certificate", would later translate into a job interview with a world-known microfinance institution, one of the best in the continent by then and perhaps now. The first interview went well and I was invited for the second interview. I knew by the end of the second interview that I had the job already; the interview was far better than I expected as I engaged the executives very much, putting forward a strong case for why I was the best candidate, never mind that I had no certificate except good "school leaving certificate" which tends to describe general behaviour. The same week I got the good news, and earning over 13,100 Kenya shillings (equivalent to approximately UK sterling £100, in December 2017 exchange rate) per month as my first salary was a very big achievement in 1994, at least I had no post high school certificate but one was being worked on in months to come. Bank clerks used to start with around 8,000 Kenya shillings and so did qualified accountants. The success after a long journey was very inspiring. Landing a job was not only due to luck but was also a God-given chance, and fitted into my new life in the city.

19

It was a challenge combining CPA studies and work but both were quite interesting since I was young and eager to learn. CPA studies complemented my work and vice versa. While pursuing CPA studies in the then Strathmore College of Accountancy (SCoA), now Strathmore University, in the capital, Nairobi, I took a critical analysis of my evening studies, given the busy work and studying life. I picked one subject and decided to try reading ahead on my own. I cannot quite remember the exact subject. From researching and trials, it was evident that the approach of personal studies enabled me to learn much faster than attending classes. This breakthrough would later allow me to study CPA via distance learning until I successfully completed it in 1999; as a result of this breakthrough my second book to be published also in December 2017 will have the title *"The Successful Distance Learning Adventure"*.

I approached SCoA and explored using distance learning materials instead of attending the hectic evening classes. It was cheap and would enable me to maximise my time, research even harder, and work hard but smartly, knowing that I did not have the luxury and advantage of attending classes like my other learning mates. My emerging strategy worked and it was interesting because during weekends I would at times be solving questions for my colleagues who carried on with the evening classes. The turning point of my distance learning strategy would pay off in June 1997 when, to my big surprise, I had emerged top student nationally in Kenya in the Company Law Prize (June 1997). The award was given by the law firm Murdoch, McCrae & Smith in the presence of the then secretary for the Kenya Accountants and Secretaries National Examinations Board (KASNEB), perhaps the most strict exam board in Kenya; winning the prize was a big achievement given that I disliked English, especially the theoretical nature of the

English language, but this reminded me of my passion for law and my ambition to study law which never materialised after high school.

The Prize really endorsed my strategy of distance learning and in June 1999 I completed my CPA (K) and in November 1999 graduated with a Bachelor of Science (BSc) with minors in mathematics and geography. By the time I graduated in November 1999, I had already secured my first expatriate job working in Hargeisa, Somaliland, as Project Accountant for a European-funded microfinance institution, established by the Nairobi-based internationally well-known microfinance institution called K-Rep, which years later transformed into a fully-fledged bank, The K-Rep Bank. I left K-Rep in November 1995 to start my bachelor's degree and leaving K-Rep to join university took the intervention of my brother and top executives in K-Rep to leave the good paying job and start university studies; it was a good decision since many good things happened after my degree studies in Nairobi.

While I pursued my bachelor's degree I was also studying for CPA and sometimes working part-time in my elder brother's business in Nairobi. My bank account was modestly loaded and I paid all my university fees without a penny from my parents; as a matter of fact I easily paid off lunch bills for working class in Nairobi despite being a hustler from rural Kenya. In fact, I was a net contributor of finances to my family right from the moment I stepped out of high school in 1994. By God's grace, it is twenty-three years since 1994 and I have never lacked anything; in fact, since high school I was on six-digit salary in Kenyan currency but always worked abroad. I may not have grown much richer than I would possibly have wished, especially if I took short cuts to prosperity, but my God-fearing nature is another side of my story which I hope to address at some point in this real life story, a long journey into The Diaspora.

Sometimes I actually wonder when I would be the net receiver of financial help, and sometimes I feel a bit scared it could be on my death bed. But I am a firm believer in giving, even though this biblical gift was nearly derailed in my long journey in The Diaspora in incidences where I lost big money back in homeland, but I did come through it triumphantly and never gave up being a giver rather than a receiver.

My university studies were exciting; better than the hustling as a result of combining day jobs and evening classes and indeed far better than high school, even though, quite frankly, in the three settings I still feel the taste of bread was much better in high school—some would argue that when a resource is scarce it tastes better since it is not available every day.

My high school was quite good and I worked very hard, as already aforementioned. My parents worked hard too to take me through high school and paid all my fees on time though quite often in instalments. I recall that many times I would go with high school fees that was just about enough to convince the school authorities to keep me in school to study despite not paying full school fees in advance. I was never sent off right away to bring fees balance in high school even before the classes began; my high school administration were quite accommodative and understanding. But my parents were very smart and would normally arrive with the fees balance just when school administration was running low in funds and about to send those with fees balances back home. Actually my parents and I had arranged such that they would either bring the fees balance on visiting day or I would collect it at half term. My mum is amazing and my late dad, who passed on in

June 1996, remains my hero and mentor. He had all the qualities everyone needs from a dad, granddad, uncle, brother, and guardian.

Because of success in private studies via distance learning, the success nearly put me in trouble in my geography classes in the university. I used to skip theoretical classes and appear only in practical sessions and exams. At some point, I was scoring very highly despite missing classes and studying privately. I was summoned by one of my geography professors and given a verbal warning about missing classes. I was reminded that attendance of lectures must be at least seventy per cent, if my memory is correct. I obliged without contesting since I knew I was wrong and had gambled too much, perhaps excessively. Apart from this isolated incident, my university life was very good; I had lots of friends and few but very close female friends. I was not really a party animal but kept several friends though had very close relationship with a few, and the relationship was really like brother-sister, brother-brother, or sister-sister in nature. I had social and business (professional) friends even though my interaction with business (professional) friends remained stronger than social ones – the reason being I was dead serious with studies and business friends fitted into this fit-for-purpose model by then.

Occasionally I would join my social and professional friends in street protests to defend fundamental freedoms in our country, Kenya. I still recall like it was yesterday an incident where President Daniel Arap Moi, the second president of the republic of Kenya, was passing near the university hostels and some rowdy students started throwing stones, only for presidential guards to cock guns out, ready to shoot so as to protect the president; by then Kenya was still struggling with multi-party democracy, reintroduced in 1991. The president stepped out of his car and with his charming skills calmed down university students, held a long chat, fatherly chat, and interestingly, out of that nearly ugly incident, he promised to join university students for dinner. Interestingly, the president would later join the University of Nairobi in the evening dinner, just few weeks later. Perhaps that was the most interesting political dinner I have ever had. We had plenty of food that the president had sponsored. Daniel Arap Moi was the second president of the republic of Kenya who ruled for twenty-four years as president, he remains a great ex-president who forged peace against all odds and is commonly called "professor of Kenyan politics".

Quite often university students would be protesting about many things that went wrong in the political, social, and economic fabric of the country and President Moi, by virtue of his position as the president, was the chancellor of all public universities. In Kenya, the universities were run by vice chancellors since the president was by default the public universities chancellor.

In my graduation on 30 November 1999, President Moi was there and one of the most treasured graduation declarations was when the president, in full gowns of presidential standard, would say "By my authority and that of the university council, I give you the power to read, write, and do all that appertains to that degree." Indeed those are extremely powerful and memorable words our late dad emphasised long before my graduation that education is so powerful and the most treasured asset one would ever have. In The Diaspora, education remains a very powerful soft power. We know that long ago education was used as a tool to regress minority people and such practices, if they still exist anywhere in the world, need serious banning.

Major industrialised economies and developed countries have succeeded because of advanced education systems. Education will remain a finite and powerful asset and there is nothing else to take that position. Poverty, disease, and ignorance are best eradicated through education. As Tony Blair, one of the best Prime Ministers of Great Britain during my time in Great Britain, once said in his speech "Education, Education, Education", that declaration was the most appropriate and correct. Without a good education system, a country can easily decline or become a net importer of human resources which then unsettles the cultural status quo in any country, and let us be honest, everyone always protects national interests first and many honest politicians of multi-national or multicultural background will attest to this fact. When president Trump says "America First" somehow I get this having been an immigrant in USA and having had close relationships with great American friends; even in my household I say "family first". Immigration is indeed a consequence of economic expansion that does not keep in pace with educational expansion. The countries that keep mourning about immigration just need to invest more in educational expansion and the subject of immigration will fizzle out. Immigration, emigration, and The Diaspora are indeed closely related.

Decision making and choices have consequences

Decision making is perhaps the most important element in human life. Decisions have consequences and so do choices. This basic concept I learnt so early in my life as described already. If I may quote the famous "choices have consequences" diplomatic spat in Kenya, following post-election violence in Kenya in 2007, when in 2012 the international diplomatic community warned Kenyan voters against choosing President Uhuru and Deputy President William Ruto in the general elections. The diplomats had warned that, should Mr. Uhuru and Mr. Ruto ascend to the presidency despite being in the International Criminal Court (ICC) case, then Kenya would suffer diplomatically and perhaps, by extension, economically and politically. "Choices have consequences" became famous words in Kenya and indeed internationally. Uhuru and Ruto were acquitted by the ICC after which Kenya saw a large number of state visits such as that by the pope (Pope Francis) and retired US president Barack Obama. But it is true that choices, decision making, and consequences go hand in hand either in a big way publicly or even privately – and it does not matter status in life, the concept cuts across.

In my journey to The Diaspora, I have had to face many decisions and choices. Success or failure in life is to a large extent determined by decision making and the choices we make. It is interesting what comes first between decision making and choices.

Decision making and choices are used interchangeably. Choice involves making a decision, but choices quite often come before a decision is made. A choice is a preference for something using a wide variety of criteria that can range from simple factors to large and complex factors. Decision making is the process of taking a stand on some selection and can be made in stages, from initial to final decisions.

The most challenging stage of choice and decision making is the consequences, or impact, which can last from minor impacts to major impacts, sometimes life changing. Some choices and decisions are permanent and irrevocable. In the modern world we have seen people change gender, and the consequences have been permanent and irrevocable.

In my life in The Diaspora, choices and decision making have been my best friends. Quite often in interviews, employers normally want to know how I made decisions and choices. Decision making and choices we make can easily tell so much about ourselves as individuals, and by the way this affects everyone in society and many times we have seen even senior people such as a minister, cabinet secretary, president or even prime minister come under sharp criticism and public scrutiny for poor and appalling decisions.

Choices and decision making can be the boundary between success and failure, prosperity and stagnation, richness and poverty, life and death, man or woman, freedom or restrictions, and other contrasts.

Biblically, God allowed choices despite even having the capability to influence human ways. Right from the Garden of Eden, God gave man and woman the liberty to make choices, but elaborated the consequences of choices. Therefore, even the Bible talks of choices having consequences.

Politically people must be allowed the opportunity to make choices otherwise there is always a risk of revolution and self-determination to push for choices of self-determination. As a write this book, many countries are re-thinking their strategic models from contested elections and referendums. Examples include polarised Kenya after recent elections, Brexit in the UK, nuclear ambitious North Korea, "America First" under President Trump, Germany with challenging coalition government or back to elections and other geo-politics of ever changing nature. Most countries have a challenge of its own.

The push for civil liberties and emergent strategy

Life in university was very good and marked a very important time in civil liberties. As university students in the capital, Nairobi, we were a force to reckon with, though perhaps not a very militant group compared to groups a decade earlier who had to pass through National Youth Service (NYS) training before joining public universities; in the United States, draft calls ended on 27 January 1973. Draft started in the United States military in 1940 when President Roosevelt signed the Selective Training and Services Act into law. This was necessary for people to fill in positions that could not be filled via voluntary means and was thus a way of enhancing national security.

Kenyan public universities, especially university student associations, have played role in boosting liberty and freedom and helped neutralise possible police brutality. In the 1990s some university students in Kenya lost up to three academic years due to the struggle for human rights, rule of law, and freedom. The brother I follow lost two years while my elder sister lost three years during political struggles of the early 1990s.

Not many universities have been proactive in the national arena and the University of Nairobi is historic as it led the way in fighting for fundamental human rights and freedoms. University closures in the 1990s were very frequent and made students lose time in fighting for civil liberties. The leader of official opposition in Kenya, Hon. Raila Odinga, is one of the most important people in the 1990s fighting for civil liberties. University students too, who equally believed in a free Kenya, joined forces with pro-democracy groups to compel the administrations of the time to respect fundamental human freedoms. The 2017 election in Kenya has made Kenyan people recall the political struggles of the 1990s which earned the term "second liberation". The first liberation was the struggle for independence from Britain, the former colony of Kenya. The third liberation arguably centres on trying to build a just country with equal opportunities, rule of law, and zero corruption. The scope of this book is not to discuss political liberations but to focus on The Diaspora.

The largest slum in sub-Saharan Africa is claimed to be the Kibera slums in the capital, Nairobi; the emergence of the slums was driven by massive rural-to-urban migration in search of opportunities. Political instability can disrupt learning and the brief overview of political instability in Kenya is meant to describe how one can manage to forge ahead by ignoring political noise and working around it to ensure steady progress. This story forms part of the journey to The Diaspora. Furthermore, lack of equal opportunities, too much corruption in public affairs, and lack of firm rule of law was the main reason I left for the adventure into The Diaspora, first as an educational migrant and later as an economic migrant.

With success before enrolling in university, I thought the frequent university closures would affect my academic studies and this compelled me to work even harder in my accountancy studies. So my life was still busy even after universities were closed due to struggle for justice and freedom.

The university students in Kenya have played a significant role in political development in Kenya. It provided massive boost for the pro-democracy movement in the frontlines who put their lives in danger. University students were and are still feared by police. University students related like a big and extended family, where a mess on one meant messing with everyone, and every administration knew and still knows the shock and awe of university students. When frustrated by the system, we had the capacity to stop Nairobi functioning, thus forcing some political concessions. It was fun using the famous "comrade power", an extremely powerful revolution. In fact, if people of any nation were to act like University of Nairobi students and students of other public universities in Kenya in the 1990s, such groups of people could force any administration to either back down or give way to a determined revolution.

It was amazing in the university how consensus on national issues was unanimous, thus creating a massive force that no one could contain. The only way for administration to calm down the situation was to call the university vice chancellor to force indefinite closure of the universities. By then, the president was the chancellor of public universities and could easily patronise the vice chancellor.

Savings to use in The Diaspora as an investment

I never had an intention or ambition to ever be part and parcel of The Diaspora. In fact, leaving for The Diaspora was an afterthought and emergent strategy before I left my initial homeland; my desire, if I ever emigrated, was actually to further my studies and return to Kenya to work, but once in The Diaspora, I reviewed my position on my preferred place. I had an ambition to pursue a Master of Business Administration degree (MBA) which developed after my first job in the university. This was driven by many job adverts in Kenya which quite often stated that "Possession of a master's degree would be an added advantage". In a competitive job environment, I always strategized to stay ahead of other competitors. I tried several scholarships after my undergraduate degree in November 1999 and the closest I came to was the University of Maastricht scholarships in the Netherlands. As a strategist, hardened by the determination to succeed, I always had a plan B in life in case Plan A failed.

After university studies, I immediately secured a job to work in Hargeisa, Somaliland. Sometimes I became too strict with myself. I recall that after I secured the Hargeisa job, my mum was tipped off about my itinerary and I was quite puzzled to see my mum among the family members to see me off in my first international assignment; interestingly, I had spoken to her nearer to my departure but she did not tell me she would be coming. I was torn between celebrating my mum's presence in Jomo Kenyatta International Airport (JKIA) and questioning whether it was a prudent surprise trip to JKIA Nairobi, which is approximately 210 kilometres from our rural home in Nakuru County. My mum well understood my strict principles of zero tolerance to wastage. As a family we had come a long way and I thought perhaps there was no time to celebrate, that the long road to success had just started. I fully understood my mum's surprise presence in JKIA; as a fifth-born, perhaps the first one to board an aircraft to a distant land, I fully understood the excitement. I still recall the great smile and hearty wave as I boarded the humanitarian flight via Djibouti to Hargeisa, Somaliland.

It was while in Somaliland that I fell in love with the United States of America. It was extraordinary time and as a political university student two years earlier, I saw a manifestation of the extremity of nations. In Kenya, President Daniel Arap Moi was facing a vote of no confidence a few years earlier while Bill Clinton in the United States was having the publicly known difficult time in the White House. As a university student, stubborn about leaving my motherland, I developed a great desire to travel to far-distant lands and the United States was a good choice. By then, President Bill Clinton had made the USA a dream country to visit. I planned my USA trip in my expatriate room in Hargeisa, Somaliland, discreetly arranging preparatory meetings in my last six months before leaving Somaliland.

By the time I completed two years in Hargeisa, Somaliland, with a Kenya-based and headquartered microfinance institution, K-Rep, I had saved enough money to take me through a full year of tuition and cost of living in the United States.

Finally I left JKIA for the United States and it was one of the longest journeys I have ever had, a long journey to The

Diaspora. The route was Nairobi-Addis-Cairo-Amsterdam-(overflew New York)-Tennessee-Oklahoma. Interestingly, I was the first international student to arrive in Oklahoma City University in the USA for the fall semester on 16 August 2001. Three weeks later, on 11 September 2011, the terrorist attack happened in America. While the nation was in shock, I was still asleep, and my Tanzanian college mate, with whom I shared a two bedroomed flat, woke me up to watch the unprecedented events in American history and the history of the world. We stared at the TV the whole day, watching as America was in crisis mode. The university had been shut down and America was in lockdown.

We watched every step of President George W. Bush, which included, apparently, Air Force One cruising above the standard 40,000 feet above the sea level, then descending into an underground runway in Nevada. President Bush was later to return to the White House, and quite frankly it was hard to see the president on TV due to multiple Marine One and escort helicopters designed to give the president of the free world unprecedented maximum security the world had never witnessed. This happened just three weeks after I landed in the United States and made us newly arrived immigrants very anxious and confused of our future time in the free land. I had just started driving when I arrived in America and on 11 September 2001, everyone in America was dashing to the gas (fuel) station to fill up the vehicles with gas (fuel)—I wondered where Americans thought they could drive to in a national emergency. The same day, there was a federal authority news brief warning gas stations not to increase fuel even by a single dime. The free land of America for once implemented emergency decrees to manage the emerging crisis. For me, while I stood by our American brothers, it was scary as a new immigrant arriving in the USA. A few weeks later, America

33

returned to normality and Americans never changed and were as good as they have always been. But of course the world changed much after 11 September 2001, and The Diaspora is the group that felt it all and immigration rules changed and overwhelmed lawyers. The challenges of life had somehow prepared me for the unexpected start of life in America.

Adventuring with ambition

My trip to America was really exploratory, driven by some undefined ambition. I needed the MBA badly but by then, anything American was prestigious. By then there was no need to emphasise "America first", since the USA was extremely powerful and was the Silicon Valley of the world, and engaging the world in extraordinary ways. Recent technological advances around the world, including the money transfer transformation in Nairobi, were yet to be conceived.

In The Diaspora, my life in the USA was very nice. I have had strange moments when I reflected about America and how far my family and relatives were across the oceans. The only people I knew before arriving in the USA were near the east coast, such as the state of New Jersey, away from the lovely Oklahoma I lived in. I made great friends in America including a very lovely African American girl who I disappointed so badly that she went on a phone call to her mum. Indeed, The Diaspora is a place of cultural shock; my great friend had misread our close association. She did tell me in her honest belief that men of African origin were taught not to date African Americans. She remained a great friend and we had deep conversations and she would weeks later tell me she was so pleased to have identified a nice boyfriend, perhaps after I said I was engaged to a lady back in Africa. I did wish her luck from the bottom of my heart. I made so many American friends and we enjoyed each other's company and for African American friends we had great stories exchanging our cultural backgrounds.

Before I left Kenya I had just dated my current wife even though we never spent much time together. I knew her while in my brief visits to Nairobi from Rest and Recuperation (R&R) trips in the capital, Nairobi. Interestingly, when I finally knew my wife's background, it happened that we had relationship via step-grandparents and one of the questions that came much later was whether we could legally marry in the African tradition. My late grandmother on my mother's side did talk to me and said she was extremely pleased I was to marry my wife because in African tradition when great-grandchildren, especially of step-great-grandparents, marry they consider the relationship as completing the puzzle and the circle—we took this to mean two families closely related historically get reunited in marriage. We were so pleased when my grandmother broke the news, otherwise it would have been too late to go back to the drawing board.

I finished my MBA studies in America and soon after crossed to England to join my current wife, my girlfriend then. She was to join me in America but it was extremely hard to get work permits in America by then and one of my sworn policies in life was never ever to remain illegal in any land around the world. Instead of being illegal, I would have preferred to fly overnight back to my country, Kenya. I had sworn to do anything with the help of Almighty God to ensure that I remain legal. In actual fact, my current wife was to join me in the USA, but I asked her to go to England for further studies. The decision for her to go to England was a well thought of and forward-looking investment. My parents had taught me that family is the best and most guaranteed insurance and this still remains my firm belief.

Justice, equality, quality of life, survival, and rule of law

On 1 October 2003 I crossed from the United States to enter the United Kingdom. It was a journey I was looking forward to as I was to meet my then-girlfriend but now-wife for the first time since August 2001, which was after two years. She had entered the UK in January 2003 to pursue undergraduate studies. Initially she was to join me in the US but once in America I changed my mind, primarily because I thought the US was too far from Kenya, my original country. The two years had moved very quickly and it was really difficult leaving behind the friends I had made in the USA, including my fellow immigrants, whom we had successfully explored the world together. My decision to move on was extraordinary and shocked many of my colleagues but I was not surprised since I had learnt the art of The Diaspora since a young age.

If there is one thing I appreciated in the USA, it was experiencing the life in the USA myself rather than being told or reading from the media. I enjoyed every bit of it and would love to return to America, even if on a visit.

The UK gave me a chance to explore life in one of the most successful empires the world still puzzles about. The UK is two and a half times smaller than Kenya, yet at one point in history the UK managed around twenty-five per cent of the world by land mass. The UK occupied the Americas before the United States gained its independence, and perhaps this is the reason why the USA and UK tend to have a special relationship.

Back in the University of Nairobi where I studied geography I did not quite manage to learn so much about other countries, since at the university level geography is more sophisticated than the word itself and is not just about mastering the atlas of the world; I remember before Iraq war not so many Americans could point to where Iraq is located. University studies in geography were not about the geographic location of a country, but more spatial topics of interest to humanity. I still recall the amazing words in geography which I found very inspirational that would later inspire me so much in life. Geography is full of big words such as "spatial", "temporal", and "paradigm shift". Spatial means relating to space, temporal means relating to time, and paradigm shift means a fundamental change in approach or underlying assumptions. It is as though the three words in geography influenced my approach to issues of the day in the space I would be in a certain time after carefully going through assumptions. My next journey after Kenya was to the United States and later to Britain, the UK.

To assist readers of this book please find **Slide 3** which charts my global movements in The Diaspora. Stories about adventures in The Diaspora will continue below. The Diaspora has taught me that every country matters and this became strikingly evident when I was in the UK.

If there is one thing that I think has made the UK a successful country it is a mixture of rule of law and its industrious past. The rule of law and economic prosperity are intertwined and one supports the other. Across the world, many people still recall the colonial governors and masters who did their job pretty well. There is no way the UK could have occupied twenty-five per cent of Earth's land mass if it did not observe the rule of law. Indeed, the UK is responsible for land demarcation of many countries today. As a religious person, I have had the privilege to read the Bible, and indeed the UK occupied the top position in the world for special reasons that are not within the scope of this book. Even if some may be unhappy about the UK's past and future success, the bad news is that part of history remains divine just as is the founding of the UK and the USA as two independent countries with special relationship; there are things that happen and happen for a reason and mankind has no control over them, no matter how large the efforts we put in as humans.

Upon landing in the UK, what puzzled me first was the underground train system, and every time I am away from the UK, then return back and use the Tube (another word for the underground system), I marvel at the whole system; the daily users in London may mourn about the tube but they forget it forms a very special underground life of London, the most amazing city on Earth. Apparently it was used as bunkers during the Second World War when Germany invaded the UK. I took the train from Heathrow to North London, then used a bus to reach where my wife was staying. All the houses in given locations looked similar and I almost asked my wife how one would know one's home; of course I knew that each house has a house number, especially from the famous 10 Downing Street, the most famous street address in the world, the official residence of UK Prime Ministers. The UK seemed greener than Oklahoma City which I had left few hours earlier.

In a few weeks, I settled in the UK as a freshman and it was time to get down to business. By then, I had used the "working holiday maker" visa that the UK government was giving to citizens from commonwealth countries. I was indeed among the first ones to use the visa in 2003. To me, the visa was really a working holiday maker visa since I learnt so much about the world while in the UK; in fact, when I applied for the UK working holiday maker visa in Los Angeles, I stated that I wanted to leave for the UK to join my partner, as well as to tour the UK to learn more about the fascinating history that shaped lots of things in our world. When one is in the USA, it is rare to hear about the outside world unless one tunes into international news channels, though this may not be the case if one is in commercial and political capitals like New York, Washington, D.C., and other cities. America is quite a self-contained country that can exist even in isolation if it wants to. The UK is quite different and as an immigrant from Africa, the

UK was a perfect place for my wife and I. In the UK, we could get all the food we would normally have in Kenya.

The special ties and special relationship between the UK and Kenya made our stay in the UK an easier one. My wife and I's family background has lots of ties to the UK. Just after independence, our parents formed a very big group and acquired land jointly from former settlers who had decided to move on, not sure if it was back to the UK or to other parts of the world. By then land was consolidated and well organised like in the rural Britain of today. All the design done in Kenya before independence was either not followed precisely or altered after independence, which then lowered agricultural production over the years. From 2002, after the long-time single political party was removed from power, Kenya started progressing economically but by then I was out of Kenya already and a self-exiled economic immigrant.

What puzzled me as well in the UK were the small roads compared to American roads, where "small roads" means all roads except dual carriageways and motorways. When I bought our first car on arrival in the UK, I had lots of issues like parking, and even driving was a challenge. In some instances I thought I would hit cars driving in the opposite direction in single carriageways. It took me nearly one month to get used to UK life. The cities are very organised and even though the housing system is communally friendly, I was later to learn that neighbours would actually not know each other except by choice really—I think people just like privacy, not that they choose not to be social.

I got to learn the UK system slowly and left the UK for abroad in November 2005, but returned back to the UK in September 2007; indeed, once a person tastes UK life it becomes contagious. One can complain about UK life but once outside the UK, it is easy to be homesick and not even the weather changes the unique nature of UK life. Even though I learnt chartered accountancy (ACCA) between 2007 and 2009, it took me long to understand the UK system because the UK is governed by a lot of laws. My focus then really was on immigration since as an immigrant I needed to remain legal since the UK is a country with very strict rule of law, as aforementioned.

Past strategies I had used, as described earlier, became quite handy and helpful. I got my first few jobs to keep me going and ensure I earned a living and kept going. My wife was still studying her undergraduate degree. I started applying for jobs while getting to learn the UK system. In summary, the UK system is organised, public facilities in the UK are well maintained, and the government makes continuous improvements. Access to public services is on First Come, First Served (FCFS) basis and there is no bending of rules or bribing your way out, as still happens in some countries. Receiving or giving bribes is outlawed and those caught doing so face the full force of the law, including a date in the jails.

Success in my prior jobs even before entering the UK was largely propelled by volunteer or internship jobs that I started off with in earlier careers. I treasure volunteering or internship. One of the first things I did in the UK was to find an internship placement organisation. Luckily I found one in London and after phone conversation, I attended an interview. I paid internship placement fees and I secured an internship role as Finance Assistant with the Mandarin Oriental hotel in Hyde Park. The hotel has visitors from around the world which boosted my adventure in The Diaspora.

I enjoyed the internship and the hotel covered my transport costs. Lunch was free and it was pretty excellent food. I enjoyed all lunches and ate my favourite fish, salmon, daily. It was a very lively office and I learnt quite a lot. It was interesting reconciling the hotel income on a daily basis. I had signed the internship for six months but on the third week of the internship, I had already secured my first paid job in the UK. I worked as a stock control assistant for Tibbet and Britten UK, which was bought by Exel Plc and later acquired by DHL. It was an exciting position and every day was an exciting day, and no day was the same as any other. I was in the administration department, ensuring that the facility worked efficiently to meet customer orders. The organisation supplied imported clothes from the facility in North London. The UK economy was extremely strong in 2004, perhaps "the boom years" as politicians in the UK love to call it. In the Prime Minister Question Time on Wednesday the words "boom" and "bust" were used so much, perhaps overused in some instances. But as a new immigrant in 2003, I quite recognised the "boom" with the "bust" coming after the 2008 global financial crisis, but quite frankly the bust may not have happened. From 2007, when I started working in the UK for the second time, to 2016, the skyline of London, the UK capital, changed dramatically. Modern buildings have emerged and life has become vibrant. Indeed economic prosperity, political stability, and rule of law are intertwined and the UK leads the world in this, just as it led the world during the industrial revolution.

In summary, the rule of law in the UK is largely responsible for the prosperity the UK has seen as an empire that has lasted perhaps much longer than many others. The UK has become more multinational, largely because of the reach of the UK in earlier years, decades, and centuries past; and this diversity is what makes the UK very successful in all spheres of life. The

UK is perhaps the most generous country that gives billions of pounds in international aid every year. In times of national challenges, the UK comes together as a nation to help. Brexit was unprecedented and even though there is worry about the impact of Brexit, the UK can still do very well even outside the European Union. Of course it would be good for the UK to remain in the EU, but the UK could still reinvent itself in the world, especially if backed up by the USA and nations of the commonwealth. There are many strategies to do this including reaching out to emerging countries that believe and practice the rule of law, the trademark of the UK.

Quite often the UK has been criticised for its colonial past but the criticism, while having some merit on past human rights grounds, does ignore the many benefits that the UK spread around the world, including its amazing record in international development. It is a fact that prior colonies of the UK have done much better compared to colonies of other nations. Just the spread of English as a business language is often overlooked by those wanting to ignore facts. The UK was the first country to ban slavery, and equal opportunities remain a priority in the UK, despite isolated cases that could be breaching equal opportunities, for which the law is robust.

Traditionally, nations that have followed the UK system, especially equality, rule of law, and parliamentary democracy, have been able to develop much faster. Emerging countries that believe in the extraordinary values of the UK have a chance to develop much faster than countries struggled to develop in the past. The values I have seen in the UK are many and include parliamentary democracy, supremacy of the parliament, rule of law, equal opportunity, openness, dynamism, generosity, and other forward-looking values.

Understanding of the Bible

It is while working and living in the UK that, for the first time, I managed to understand the Bible well, more than at any time ever since. A work colleague in one of the multinational companies I worked for used to distribute some fliers for United Church of God, a church organisation based in Cincinnati in Ohio, United States. One day he gave me one flier which I read and then subscribed for free booklets which used to be dispatched from a distribution centre in London; some of the booklets came directly from Ohio to my address in Britain. In my adventure in The Diaspora, the moment I understood the Bible well remains the most important moment, since for a long time I tried to search a lot about the Bible. The year was 2004.

It was puzzling to learn that the reason the Kings James Version (KJV), or Kings James Bible (KJB) or Authorised Version (AV), is called King James is because it is an English translation of the Bible for the Church of England. The translations started in 1604 and ended in 1611 and were the third and last translation by the Church. The translation made a big impact around the world, since English was already the business language and will remain so for a very long time to come, perhaps until the next world. The Bible is indeed the most popular book ever and has had a big impact in English-speaking nations of the world, especially the British Commonwealth of Nations, the nations that could easily work out big trade deals with the UK after exit from the EU.

For me being able to dig deep into the Bible in the UK was unprecedented because as young children in Africa we used to be given small bibles for free, especially by the European missionaries. When I was young the Bible, especially the New Testament handed to us, was very handy. I must admit that I never understood the Bible well, especially the contents. The Bible is a very complex book to understand but the internet has made many things quite easy. But there is no other materials I have come across that better explains the Bible more than the booklets distributed by United Church of God based in Cincinnati, Ohio. The materials are outstanding because it is based on facts around the world. It is hands on, not just Biblical theories.

It was only after I left the multinational company in the UK that I began to appreciate the help my work colleague had given me. By handing me the flier for United Church of God he made a big difference in my life. In fact, I was so inspired that I read the entire Bible, both Old and New Testament, while commuting to work via train in the UK in 2015. I read the entire Bible in less than one year and made my own notes. It was a lifetime dream come true and I will forever thank my work colleague for reaching out. In the near future, I will share my notes on the internet once I complete editing and will include a link to this book.

In life there are many things to pass over to young generations, and it takes many forms such as stories, wealth, debt, mortgage, education, property, books, and other gifts. I am sure many people treasure receiving free wealth, property, and other gifts of monetary value. But I think the most important and long lasting gifts to pass over to young generations are education and the Bible, especially for Christians. Education is an intangible asset and so is what we learn from reading the Bible. The Bible is tangible but the benefits that come from reading the Bible are intangible and long lasting.

When we were growing up our parents emphasised the need to adhere to biblical practices and principles and explained to us the benefits and importance of observing God's words. It was not forced and we reserved the right to take note or leave it. I am pleased that in my journey in The Diaspora I was able to experience this in a great way. Just as we received this gift from our parents, we have learnt to explain the same to our children—this is a gift that every Christian parent ought to explain to their children.

The Bible is priceless and enduring in this world and definitely into the next world. The Bible strengthens one's faith, and I encourage every Christian to be steadfast in understanding our God.

Explaining the Bible is not within the scope of this book but I may, from time to time, write separate articles regarding the Bible.

Original home versus The Diaspora and impact of global village

The world has changed dramatically since the accelerated inventions in technology. I still remember the annoying and expensive dial-up internet immediately before the start of the twenty-first century, around 1999 to 2000, and the quite dense mobile phones; I was so privileged to have held the first of them in Africa, courtesy of my well-off elder brother. There was no broadband then. The WhatsApp of today (started January 2009) was years away and Skype (started in August 2003) was possibly in its final stages in Silicon Valley. Bible scholars, who happen to include myself, believe that accelerated technology and travel signify the latter days when the fall of man will be as profound as during the days of the Ark of Noah.

Human beings are naturally social and one of the biggest questions of unprecedented global movements has been the well-being of the family. Everyone desires close family relationships and the big question remains how to keep family intact whilst enjoying the fruits of globalisation.

Quite often, I come across very successful families in many countries who passionately talk about the global reach they have as a family, which could be a product of political or economic migration and subsequent social migration. Global migration has always been driven by both political and economic migration, with social migration usually following earlier economic or political migration. Social migration is where families move from one place to another so as to join earlier migrants known to them. Social migrants usually face the biggest challenge because of the tightening of immigration laws and rules.

In my opinion, globalisation and technological advances have made a case for The Diaspora. Most barriers to global mobility have been overcome by ever-improving technology.

The old headache of whether to live in The Diaspora or move to the original homeland has been bypassed by advances in technology. But technology is becoming an enemy of face-to-face touch since it is common these days for children to ignore the old forms of socialism and opt for electronic socialism. Parents must play a big role to reduce electronic socialism and encourage the traditional face-to-face socialism, especially among children.

The changes since my first adventure to The Diaspora in 1994 and then around 1999 are, by contrast to this year, 2017, so significant. In fact, if there is anybody who is afraid of adventuring in The Diaspora legally, then these are unfounded fears. The world has moved on and The Diaspora continues to be a global village with falling walls and barriers of years past.

Values and norms

Values and norms may differ across people, counties or cultures. But there are universal or generally accepted values and norms. Surviving in The Diaspora requires adherence to values and norms of the host communities. Adherence does not mean following the rules blindly, but having a cross and sense check to ensure new values and norms are consistent with general and universal principles. It is always good to have an open mind and not be closed to accepting new things, as long as it does not violate the generally accepted values and norms. But there is misconception about the West. When I landed in America I expected to see an extremely liberal society, perhaps a replicate of the extremes were see in the Television sometimes. A good example is dressing and I expected to possibly find Americans dressing like we see in movies. But by contrast, I found a measured society with great values, respect for people, very hardworking, accommodative and great fun to socialise with. Some claimed I was in the slow states in the middle of America, Oklahoma, and that I never saw the fun and extreme of big cities. Interestingly, when my wife left Kenya for Britain, one of the funny jokes was that she be careful not to end up with a boyfriend somewhere. Having been in USA, I knew that life in the West was abit of cultural shock because as immigrants from Africa sometimes we read too much into Television information completely forgetting that there is a normal life, outside of the extremes of mass media and Television. But I think the rule of law makes a big difference and one area with big difference between the West and developing countries is family life. In developing countries it is easy for fatherless children to struggle in life while in the West men who father around take financial responsibility and this make men in the West to tread very carefully. Many developing countries have too many fatherless children who suffer in life and if there is a law that developing countries need to adopt quickly it is that of penalising men, who father around irresponsibly, to ensure that no child is left with no help and that men who father must take the financial and social responsibility – a very urgent legislation is needed here.

In an effort to maintain values and norms, one must not be left isolated, since values and norms affect a community of people and not just individuals. It is always therefore good to ensure that, as an individual, the values and norms practiced are consistent with those practised in a community or a community of a nation.

Social life is very important in The Diaspora and could possibly determine the pace one that learns and subsequently integrates into a new community in The Diaspora. There are plenty of opportunities to socialise in a measured way and it is always good to maximise on them.

Values and norms that are inconsistent with law should not be adopted as it may not only be illegal, but could put one in real trouble. What may be practised in one part of the world may be illegal in other parts of the world. For example, hunting as a norm in some parts of the world is outlawed in other parts.

Golden rules in The Diaspora

Being a member of The Diaspora comes with profound benefits, obligations, and responsibilities. Going into The Diaspora can be very rewarding but comes with huge cost, risk, and challenges which must be handled very well if one is to be successful—and this is the reason why I wrote this book, to be quite handy for The Diaspora. When I departed abroad to The Diaspora in 1999 there was no guide at all, but I managed to stay away well since that time to date, thanks be to God.

Being in The Diaspora can be challenging culturally since one is compelled to put up with situations and people that one would possibly have little patience for outside The Diaspora, a cosmopolitan land of diverse people. But quite often, people confuse fitting into a new culture as meaning transforming one's culture to new one, or abandoning the old culture for the new one—this is not true. Diversity is something to be celebrated, since every human being is unique and special. Cultures are equal, none superior or inferior. The only difference is cultures that do not promote the well-being of humanity or violate the rules and laws that promote cohesiveness.

It is for this reason that I outline below the golden rules of The Diaspora.
1. Observe the law and/or rule of law if in a leadership role.
2. Respect host communities.
3. Do not forget your roots or origin; remember everyone has one.
4. Be up to date with laws and regulations.

5. Avoid family breakdown unless inevitable.

6. Continuously improve oneself and make education and/or business a priority.

7. Avoid being stagnant or feeling stagnant and try to be dynamic.

8. Use magic and priceless words such as "please" and "thank you", and mean it.

9. Be assertive when necessary.

10. Maintain vital networks, especially social and professional ones.

11. Avoid stereotyping things.

12. Believe in God, observe the Ten Commandments if a Christian, or observe similar or other equivalents in other religions.

After many years in The Diaspora and having transitioned from being an immigrant into a new country, I am pleased to explain the twelve golden rules of The Diaspora. If one is to be successful in The Diaspora anywhere in the world then it is essential to observe the twelve golden rules.

In newspapers, we read the worrying stories of children drowning to reach Europe, immigrants risking their lives in the Mediterranean to reach the shores of Europe, conflicts around the world that are displacing people in large numbers, and advanced countries struggling to keep their borders under check.

For potential immigrants, it is important to be reminded that being in The Diaspora lawfully is the first, most important step. Therefore, for those trying to cross illegally, it is important to note this factor. In my journey in The Diaspora, having lived in five countries legally outside of my country of origin but having visited many other nations, I am pleased to outline what I see as twelve golden rules in The Diaspora.

1)   Observe the law and/or rule of law if in a leadership position.

To begin with, it is important to be in The Diaspora legally and indeed observe the laws. If one is illegal in The Diaspora, it is hard to regularise one's stay. Therefore, by all means, it is important to be in a place legally unless one can demonstrate (quite often with personal risks) that being in The Diaspora was a matter of life and death, which can be quite challenging, if not impossible, to prove in law.

2)   Respect host communities.

To be successful in The Diaspora, one needs to respect host communities. Respect alone has the potential to accrue a lot of benefits. With respect, one is able to gain quite useful information that assists one to succeed in The Diaspora.

But respecting host communities does not mean shying away from pursuing opportunities in life even where one has to compete with members of the host country. The newly arrived will always be disadvantaged in a way, but earlier explained strategies for success in a competitive environment become very hand in The Diaspora. The Diaspora can be the result of rural-to-urban or city-to-city migration nationally, or international migration to The Diaspora.

3)   Do not forget your roots or origin.

There is a saying in Swahili that says "*mwacha mila ni mtumwa*" which means "whoever abandons culture is a slave". Fitting into The Diaspora can be quite difficult, even with advanced social skills. In The Diaspora, normally, people are quite busy, and there is no time for anyone to guide you around, furthermore the host country for The Diaspora is multi-cultural, meaning it can be quite difficult to get people who would have similar background. In The Diaspora world, whichever country one finds oneself in, is usually an advanced place already, and sticking initially to what one is familiar with whilst trying to learn the new world is the only path to success, a slow but sure path since radical change may be unfavourable.

Furthermore, even when trying to have some paradigm shift, it is good to do it progressively and safely. Learn new tricks first, then forget old roots when safe to do so. People who get into trouble in The Diaspora are those who want radical change when it is not safe.

4)   Be up to date with laws and regulations.
Laws and regulations govern the conduct of people and exist to preserve order in public. New immigrants into The Diaspora are usually the most susceptible to changing rules and regulations and I found the need to keep up to date with laws and regulations as the most demanding but important aspect. Lawyers are very expensive in The Diaspora and quite unaffordable. This basically means that to succeed in The Diaspora, one has to be somehow their own wise lawyer and counsel. When rules change it is not the responsibility of the government to explain new laws, but whoever is governed by the new law is expected to somehow find out. Staying up-to-date with ever-changing laws and regulations is therefore very important; we know very well that ignorance of the law is not a defence.

Technological advances have made life easy, since one can Google their own way out into the latest laws and regulations. But the time spent on social media sometimes deprives us time to get updated with important information that can make or break life in The Diaspora.

5)   Avoid family breakdown unless inevitable.

Being far away from an original homeland can be very difficult socially, especially where there are extreme cases of discrimination. Discrimination varies and can be manifested socially, culturally, or even economically in terms of economic opportunities. Luckily though, discrimination, just like slavery, is forbidden in many countries where The Diaspora live, as it is a disgraceful and old vice that has got no place in human history and human life. Every man and woman was created equal before God and in the Christian religion, man was created in God's own image, therefore in the spiritual perspective, discrimination is self-defeating.

The most important source of social life remains the family, and in The Diaspora this is the most crucial aspect of social life. The family is the most simple, easy, understanding, primary, all-time, unconditional, divine, robust, reliable, nice, dreamy, and all-one-could-ask-for institution that signifies stability, togetherness, passion, and love. In The Diaspora, family comes first and everything else comes second. Without a family, unless deceased, one becomes vulnerable or secondary to others. Therefore maintaining family relationships is paramount, and biblically there are many examples, including the prodigal son; one can run away from family but ultimately return, perhaps in a more miserable and desperate state.

Family breakdown in The Diaspora is the most devastating thing. Luckily though, breakdown is quite often caused by external interference outside the family, and such interference is easily warded off in a stable family. You will have seen that on Facebook, for example, lots of people prefer to put "complicated" under their relationship status. For sure, relationship is the most important ingredient in a family, and breakdown often comes as a result of persistent strain in relationships among family members.

6) Continuously improve oneself and make education and/or business a priority.

Investment in education remains the most important decision in The Diaspora. Education is so powerful that nothing can challenge it. Education is a life in itself and provides something that is very beneficial that nobody can mess with it. With education, progress is guaranteed, since continuous improvement makes one better over time.

Business should always remain the second priority after education. But there should never be a choice between education and business since both are equally attainable, though the challenge is, of course, having the resources, time, and effort to pursue both at the same time. But pursuing education and business is even sweeter since one gets the best of both investments.

7) Avoid being stagnant or feeling stagnant and try to be dynamic.

The Diaspora can be enjoyable depending on what one does. It is easier to think that enjoying life in The Diaspora is all about having lots of money. In fact, the craving for money is always a problem since no amount of money is ever enough and the more one has, the more one wishes to have; it can be an endless craving that leaves no peace of mind, heart, and soul.

If there is a number one thing to avoid in The Diaspora, it is the state of feeling or being stagnant. This could happen because of doing the same thing throughout, having no change in reward for work or motivation to work, or being weighed down by things that constantly disturb peace of mind.

The feeling of being stagnant is not good and best way to get out of such a situation is to first reach out socially and talk about it with family and friends, and if it persists, it is better to seek advice of a qualified counsellor.

Social walls bring lots of disadvantages and easily close opportunities.

8) *Use magic and priceless words such as "please" and "thank you"—and mean it*

If there is a time and place that the magic and priceless words need to be used most then it is in The Diaspora. Relationships are the most important virtue away from a homeland, and there are only two words that can open any gates, namely "please" and "thank you". For arrogant people, "please" and "thank you" are alien words, but to the respectful, humble, and God-fearing people, these words remain a treasure, a license to success, a breakthrough, and the keys that open up opportunities. "Please" and "thank you" are perhaps the most used words in The Diaspora, followed by the usual greetings.

"Please" and "thank you" signify a way of life, a culture, and a form of respect, and signal duty of care and deep respect. They are human words that make people listen and oblige.

9)   Be assertive when necessary.

Being respectfully assertive is an indicator of a measured level of confidence, and makes one be taken seriously and with respect. The spirit and timing of assertiveness is very important. To whom assertiveness is focused really matters a lot. Being assertive is a way of expressing one's own thought in good body language.

While being assertive, it is necessary to do it with respect, good body language, in a friendly way, and with sense of humour. Being overly or excessively assertive could be misconstrued to mean arrogance, which is a very bad vice in The Diaspora.

Being assertive wards off potential opportunists who would want to use one's weakness or vulnerabilities. The Diaspora is a very competitive place and only those who adapt easily survive well.

While being assertive is very important, it should not be overused, and it can be seen as patronising, which is quite often counterproductive. When expressing a dissenting view, it is good to avoid being too assertive unless there are big concerns or stakes in question.

10)   Maintain vital networks, especially social and professional ones.

Even a non-English speaker is not likely to miss the definition of a network as an interconnection of a system or people. Networking therefore involves a system and people with convergent efforts—never divergent efforts. This book focuses on people, not systems, but we know that people create systems and not vice versa. Even though systems remain complex in nature due to their ability to work perfectly well by all measures, it is important to acknowledge that the boss of any system remains the people.

Systems exist in all disciplines from physiology, computing, geology, astronomy, and indeed other sophisticated sciences. Even when writing this book, I had to follow a systematic pattern.

Systems work well and as humans, we marvel at how systems lead to amazing things. In The Diaspora, the system works and networking is part of ensuring that one remains up-to-date.

Birds of the air know no national boundaries. Being in The Diaspora needs this kind of mind-set. One comes across many things and people, but cherry-picking the right networks helps.

One gets to learn many things, sometimes even by just observation, which is part of networking. Have you ever wondered about the similarity between aeroplanes and birds? The design of a plane is no different from the architecture of a bird. Just as birds move through taking flight, it seems the same thinking was made around planes taking off. If there is something similar between a plane and a bird, it is the take-off and landing mechanics.

If you have ever taken a flight, and I imagine most readers of this book have, you will realise some obvious mechanics. On take-off, planes seem to stretch their wings, and on landing, they open their wings, and birds do the same. Sometimes it is fair to assume that there is a high likelihood that the inventor of the plane may have studied the birds very well.

The take-off and landing of a bird and a plane involves well-coordinated and networked systems that work seamlessly. Landing and taking off well in The Diaspora really depend on one's ability to make use of social and professional networks. Despite the challenges of social and professional life, one needs extra efforts to make things work. Social and professional circles can provide a priceless minefield of useful leads, tips, advice, information, and other resources that are free of charge.

Ignoring social and professional networks in The Diaspora can be a big problem. It can be a regressive move with unfavourable outcomes. In my first adventure in The Diaspora life in Hargeisa, Somaliland, social and professional networks may not have been so crucial, like the social and professional networks I needed when I arrived in America in August 2001, just three weeks after the famous 11 September 2001. In fact, the following day after September 11th, I had an appointment in the State of Oklahoma with a career counsellor who works in the employment bureau of the state. I had gone there for a chat as part of trying to understand career development in America. Rather than hear somebody else explain to me the work situation, as a newly arrived immigrant I really wanted to hear it first-hand from a government or state employee. It was a useful conversation that gave me a lot of free and primary sources of information. Of course I never expected the federal employee to land me a job, since I knew America did not work like that; a sharp contrast to some countries around the world where you have to know somebody to get a job.

Social and professional network is something to build. It needs time, effort, dedication, and judgement. Everyone perhaps knows some stories that are very inspiring. Perhaps the most amazing one is for former US president Barack Obama. President Obama started off as a senator for Illinois and before landing a job in Illinois, Obama had taken the social trajectory of success. He built a strong social network, working hands-on with community workers with his transformational ideas. The success of Obama therefore started from very humble beginnings. Quite often we think of success in The Diaspora as about pursuing something big, the magnitude of industrial revolution. Sometimes we dream big ideas and forget the small and basic ideas that can lead to big things. In The Diaspora, it is good to maximise on the small things very smartly before moving to big things; we must not ignore the power of lessons learnt, improved learning curve, and potential for exponential growth.

Actually, in The Diaspora, many immigrants who wanted quick riches, quick fixes, and an easy life quite often find themselves at odds with the tough law in The Diaspora, and end up either in jail or being deported. In social and professional networks, we learn the basics, then trial and error before our actions matter. One learns to agree or disagree, corrections, approval or disapproval, and at times feels like it is back to school, but in the end we become wiser, respectful and respected, and most importantly, learn to live well with diverse people.

Social and professional networks are therefore a success propeller in The Diaspora, and for new people in The Diaspora this is even more crucial.

11) Avoid stereotyping things or being judgemental.
The Diaspora usually comprises very diverse people. Diversity happens in many ways, such as by culture, national

origin, religion, ability, disability, and other forms that have elements of distinction.

To work in a diverse setting, one must learn not to be judgemental as this can unsettle others, leading to conflict. There is a generally accepted premise that the best workers in international and multinational organisations are those that are never judgmental.

Being judgemental can unsettle the sensitive issues in the diverse world of The Diaspora.

12) Believe in God; observe the Ten Commandments.

Christians believe in God and are obliged to follow the Ten Commandments. Non-Christians are welcome to follow suit if it does not violate their religious views. Other religions may have their own divine rules to follow, but humanity largely believes in the same God.

Being in The Diaspora, especially when new, is never easy. Quite often, faith keeps one going. I remember that many times in America, attending church gave me peace of mind and reason to be hopeful. Working and studying is always a challenge but church provides endless nourishment.

The UK was quite dramatic for me in terms of understanding God the Almighty as aforementioned. It is while working that a colleague introduced some booklets for United Church of God (UCG). Through the materials, I learnt a lot more than at any time in my life. I have read nearly all the materials of UCG. I was already a believer, even before being introduced to UCG and before coming across UCG materials, but UCG did shed unprecedented light on the Bible, the word of God.

The purpose of this book is not to discuss religion in detail but to emphasise the fact that religion has an important and intangible benefit to mankind and especially those in The Diaspora. As mentioned already, observing the law is the most essential step in The Diaspora. The Bible states laws in the form of commandments, which are ten in number. And Jesus made it even easier by summing the commandments into the most important and greatest two commandments as written in Mark 12, namely: love your God with all your heart and mind, and then love your neighbour. Jesus did this to simplify the commandments and expressly said that these two commandments were the greatest; if one follows these two, then all other commandments would have been followed.

I have quite often attended church with non-Christians in The Diaspora and it is fun. The Diaspora usually comprises people from all denominations, and success in The Diaspora requires one to respect people of other denominations or religions. Everyone matters in The Diaspora regardless of the differences we may have, be it of nature or human making. Terrorism in any form is disgraceful and leads nowhere – it has no destiny in the modern world and in the world to come.

Terrorism is a cancer that has no place in human life. It must be rejected. Governments across the world have done well in counter-terrorism efforts, and communities in The Diaspora need to understand that success in The Diaspora is through respect for humanity. Religious leaders need to teach humanity the good old basics that kept the world safe for a long time in an effort to complement outstanding government efforts.

The world changed on 11 September 2001, when I was just three weeks in the USA. Hopefully preaching love will ultimately eradicate terrorism from the world. The Diaspora have been the most affected by the menace of terrorism, but outstanding efforts have been made in counter terrorism. Counter narrative to terrorism is something book writers need to emphasise. Knowledge is power and counter narrative to bad things in the society would be helpful especially to The Diaspora.

Entry strategy to The Diaspora

There is no universal entry strategy into The Diaspora since the migration to The Diaspora is caused by different reasons. Migration into The Diaspora can be due to social, political, or economic reasons.

The entry point usually depends on the reason for moving into The Diaspora in the first place.

If migration is for social reasons, such as to join family, then the entry point would be the place where the family is. If migration is political, chances are one would be joining family or place permitted by an approving authority.

Economic migration is really the focus of this book. Economic migrants could be either employers or employees. Employers would choose an entry point where a market exists for their products, while employees would want highly developed places where it is easy to find a job. Sometimes economic migrants end up in a new country with the assumption being that there is automatic success. What are quite often ignored are the requirements to be able to work in a new country. But for economic migrants, I guess the mind-set is always to escape away first and worry about requirements once there. It would be very interesting if governments handling immigration were to share such challenges with would-be immigrants to see whether, with more information, they would still be risking a move into the unknown.

Educational migration is moving outside one's home country to pursue further education. In the past decade, more so after the

2008 global financial crisis, there has been significant drop in educational immigration. Even without statistics to demonstrate this, it is clearly evident from tightening immigration rules and abolishment of former immigration schemes that enabled highly educated people to remain in The Diaspora countries after completing education. In the past, educational migrants used to be motivated by post-study work visas. After my MBA in the USA in 2003, I never bothered to stay much longer since it was almost impossible to get work sponsorship after a one year non-renewable post-work visa, and one of my policies then and now is never to stay in any country illegally, as this easily exposes one to problems. Furthermore, once one is illegal, it becomes hard to put forth a legal case to remain.

When I migrated from Kenya to America in 2001 to pursue my MBA, I never had the ambition of overstaying in the USA. In fact, I wanted to complete my education, do some internship, then go back to Kenya or elsewhere. Before heading off from Kenya, I did thorough research and spoke to two immigration lawyers. One of the lawyers I spoke to knew some information about immigration to Canada. He was very frank about it and explained how it may not be as rosy as some put it at that time. He clarified though that compared to developing countries, opportunities are many, but that we should not think that life will just be easy and on a silver spoon, but that one will need to work hard, perhaps even harder than back in their country of origin. That conversation put me off immigration just for the purposes of working. I then decided to first immigrate and study.

My late dad told us time and again that in the future, education would be tantamount to land as a form of capital in the good days gone past. He knew that unlike his days where one just needed to get land somewhere, sometimes free, and then life was sorted, the future would involve more education, that the most important investment would be education. My late dad indeed invested heavily, perhaps the bulk of his resources, to ensure everyone had basic education back in Kenya.

We know of false stories by The Diaspora to paint The Diaspora as a land of plenty flowing with milk and honey. Before I left for the USA, I had heard of such stories that one could afford a big house, big car, and other big things. What people quite often forget to ask is at what price. Actually, it took the sudden emergence of powerful social media for prior fake stories of rosy life in The Diaspora to be exposed. Lots of stories started emerging after 2008, perhaps triggered by global financial crisis. I thought that for would-be immigrants, this was the best news, since it is better for people to know what to expect instead of waste time, money, and efforts, then become disappointed after paying a huge price.

In fact, when I was in The Diaspora, I ensured that I did not create an impression of easy life, as this would have motivated people I knew to make unnecessary requests. Who would not want to receive free money for nothing in return? I knew some members in The Diaspora who created this impression, then ended up having to avoid people for fear of constant nagging. It is wrong for The Diaspora to create such an impression since it puts one in a tricky position in the event of needing help from back home; there is nothing good life than the truth as it is known to promote freedom, setting people free.

Related to entry strategy is the entry time. If I was to start the journey to The Diaspora afresh, knowing what I know now, I would set a time limit to enter. I left Kenya at the age of twenty-four to take my first expatriate job in Hargeisa, Somaliland. Going to The Diaspora to work right away with everything arranged by an employer is quite different from going to The

Diaspora as a self-sponsored student hustling all the way through. In 2001, I took the bold and brave move as an educational immigrant and looking back, it was perhaps the best age to take the risk. I had no responsibility then, though the economic situation in Kenya was awful then and I had to send buffer funds to help my larger family in Kenya. We were not that badly off, like average and hardworking families in Kenya, we were neither too poor to struggle nor too rich to flash the little money around. We were precisely middle class, many times richer and better-off compared to what the United Nations (UN) defines as a poverty indicator or cut-off, so in a way, I felt lucky and motivated to take a measured risk and pursue life in The Diaspora.

Heading into The Diaspora requires a young age since it is like being born again and starting life afresh. Heading to The Diaspora after thirty-five years of age is perhaps a big challenge, especially if it involves going to start off life afresh – and I hereby emphasize the word to "start off" since nobody should be discouraged. But it is not surprising to see families dispose of property and head off to The Diaspora at advanced age—in that case, this is quite different as it involves complete relocation. The best age to head off to The Diaspora alone is perhaps from early twenties to mid-thirties. My wife headed off to The Diaspora straight from college at the age of twenty-four and upon arriving in Britain, got welcomed by flu and snow weather. She seemed poorly with perhaps the first flu ever and the landlady did ask her if her mum had assented to her moving abroad. The landlady was very correct in the sense that moving to The Diaspora requires a certain age. She was indeed the best age to head off to The Diaspora.

Moving to The Diaspora at teenage age can be quite a challenge depending on upbringing. Moving to The Diaspora past a certain age can bring other challenges such as late entry into career. From experience, the best age range is twenties to thirties.

But for foreign investors there is never anything like age barriers for migration into The Diaspora. Companies as legal entities also do face barriers to entry into foreign countries, but this book focuses on individual migration into The Diaspora. Perhaps after my law studies in 2019, I will aim to publish a book on corporate migration.

Tough immigration policies in The Diaspora

As aforementioned my wife and I survived on student visas abroad long before we were granted indefinite leave to remain in the UK. At some point, I qualified for the highly skilled migrant program (HSMP) visa while I was working in Kabul, Afghanistan. The point-based system implemented by the labour government in the UK was a great plan, just like the working holiday maker visa which I used to enter the UK from the USA. While still in Afghanistan, I engaged a UK lawyer I identified online while still in Kabul. Thanks to great values in the UK, I knew that even without due diligence I could trust the UK lawyer to do his job and make submissions on my behalf. He did a brilliant job and it never cost me much, since as an expatriate I was loaded with some dollars.

I scored enough points in HSMP that reflected the true face of The Diaspora. The minimum required was over seventy-five points, which I attained easily and exceedingly due to the highest level of education I held with a masters, MBA studies (USA), earnings based on work experience (Kabul, Afghanistan), a secured UK employer that enabled me to earn sufficient points based on annual salary, and UK experience which had a few points as an additional score. So my adventure in The Diaspora in the USA, UK, and Afghanistan had counted and this made me feel good that the adventure into the unknown had produced well known and well deserved results. The strong footing I had before leaving my original homeland in Kenya played a key role in my subsequent journeys in The Diaspora. Life is indeed complicated since earning HSMP required one to have a combination of skills and experience, some of which required multi-country adventure.

HSMP was a key flagship scheme in UK immigration, comparable to the point system in Australia. Even though immigration routes was later politicised, including HSMP, it has indeed benefitted global Britain, the small country that has puzzled the world with extraordinary achievements in all spheres of life.

The journey to settlement in the UK was tough and the office administering UK immigration, the Home Office (HO), was known, if not notorious, for tough application of the rules, though quite frankly but understandably, sometimes they went overboard. In my journey in The Diaspora, I agreed to disagree and disagreed to agree with HO. The immigration fee was very high and sometimes I wonder how we managed and in the event an application was rejected, one had to sadly lose a large amount of fees. Before leaving the UK in 2005, I had attempted to apply for an independent visa via the point system but I got negative feedback and consequently, I planned to exit the UK since I never believed and still do not believe it is wise to live illegally in a country unless it is the option of the last resort, unless if one is in a fix with no system to support an exit strategy. So in 2005, I departed the UK, but returned in 2007 under HSMP; I was already used to life in Britain where lots of things are very convenient, but of course, it comes at a price since we pay our fair share of contribution in taxes. When I exited the UK in 2005, I never considered the move as a tactical retreat but a long haul exit however life has taught me to be open minded and focused. But the decision to return in 2007 via HSMP was largely informed by my MBA studies in America where we were taught that strategies can fail but individuals and corporations must gather intelligence and spot emergent strategies and seize the opportunities that come with it. The HSMP was an emergent opportunity and I deployed the best of my MBA studies to tackle the once in a life time chance and opportunity. When HSMP was discontinued in UK, I learnt that if I had stayed in Kabul for even one more month there was a chance the scheme would have been abolished before I was in.

By the time we were granted indefinite leave to remain, my wife and I were completely exhausted. We have, I believe, three box files of immigration documents in the UK alone, let alone my adventures in other countries. The UK remains one of the most dynamic and forward-looking countries in the world so the hustling we underwent to settle in Britain was an effort well-earned and deserved. This journey prompted me to write this book to document the extraordinary journey of not giving up. Hopefully this can be good testimony to many people who are battling challenges in life or are about to embark on one; even in a difficult journey forget challenging past and plan a rosy future. This narrative is a useful story to children of immigrants as it is important to know history so that the hard-earned achievements by parents are not blown away.

For those new in The Diaspora, one of the critical things to do is to keep up to date with changing rules. Immigration lawyers are quite expensive and sometimes rules change very fast. The best survival tactic is to keep up to date with changing rules, and this may mean subscribing to free updates via the internet. One can always Google and find the best sources of information.

Back in Kenya, I saw plenty of successive generations blow away the hard won success of earlier generations. For example, very elite parents would go through thick and thin to make it in life, only to be followed by careless children who blew away hard built success; there are many stories of earlier generations rising from rags to riches only to be followed by generations that know no history and care less and end up shifting from riches to rags through a series of bad and disastrous decisions and judgements. There is nothing to deter such a sad shift in fortunes than a story that tells things as they are, without beating about the bush, but setting the record straight—things should be told as they are since years of public relations have sometimes failed to show desirable results.

The low cost, high value for money

One of the fears of people around the world when it comes to venturing in The Diaspora is the tyranny of finances. Raising finances is one of the biggest challenges, but this is indeed a myth and misconception. The red tape to The Diaspora is indeed very prohibitive and expensive. The fat bank statements one is required to produce makes those with ambition to proceed to The Diaspora to just give up.

The fear of high cost of living in The Diaspora normally leads many not to even try except the brave ones who believe that it is better to try and fail rather than fail to try at all. High risk, high return is the motivator for the minority in The Diaspora rather than low risk, low return for the majority who are risk averse.

When I left for America in 2001, I had saved plenty in my first expat job, but I went the extra mile and disposed some of the investments I had that made no sense to keep by then. At the age of twenty-six, I thought I was better off knowledgeable and wiser rather than less travelled, less informed, but perhaps wealthy. My family was well-off but I am sure they could have lived comfortably with the savings I had accumulated, but I felt I needed something radical, far-reaching, and extraordinary.

At a tender age I had mastered the strategic thinking of "all options on the table". My plan to self-sponsor myself into the unknown world of The Diaspora was very much in the cards and options. But before using lots of my hard-earned savings on the unknown, I had tried several scholarships but failed. The closest I almost got was a scholarship in the Netherlands which failed after close hope and a long wait. While I awaited the scholarship decision, my plans to leave for America were at an advanced stage; it was just to press the button and I would wake up the next day in America. I was so prepared and had linked up with a host family in America from whom I rented their external room.

In fact, I was so well-prepared that I had factored in the possibility of being disappointed upon reaching America that I would make a decision to return back to Kenya almost immediately because of extraordinary disappointment with my new life in The Diaspora. I felt optimistic but I internally built a pessimistic counter-narrative to manage my expectations. My first few months were challenging and what kept me going were the modest savings I had and friends to talk to. Unlike people who are sponsored through large fundraisings and thus have massive expectations, my situation was unique and I had no pressure to report to anyone. Of course, I kept in touch with family, friends, my mum, and my girlfriend then.

My strategy even before landing in America was already well-known, that I would keep costs low but get value for money in everything I did. Extravagance is something I hate since in most cases it is tantamount to living beyond one's means. My friends and I enjoyed our stay in America. As postgraduate students we went after bargains. One such grand bargain was a weekly buffet with some friends every Sunday from afternoon to evening time in Oklahoma City. My greatest friend in America, my fellow buddy in The Diaspora from Kenya, was as skinny as a needle but could do up to three rounds of plates. Myself, I used to struggle with even a single plate. The buffet continued until I left America. The get-together to eat was a fun time, a time to forget the studies, the work, and the weekly hustling, and do something different.

Getting income in The Diaspora, especially when newly arrived, is always a challenge. Income is the hardest thing to control. But costs are easy to control since one can make affordable choices. Therefore my low cost, high value for money lifestyle was informed by restricted income opportunities for the newly arrived in The Diaspora.

A low cost strategy became my winning plan and I will forever be thankful to my parents who taught us as a family to be wise spenders. The basic virtue in life did assist me to conquer life in America and I have ever since maximised on this strategy.

One of the motivations for heading into The Diaspora was the need to ensure a sustainable living. I knew getting an expatriate job as my first job was God's gift and a great blessing and the last thing I ever wanted to happen was to fail to use the chance to do something very extraordinary, radical, and full of impact. I thought very hard about many options, including buying a flashy car or house, doing business, or just saving the money. But I needed something radical, that will just change everything and rewrite history. I explored all choices and came to the conclusion that investing in education would be the best strategy.

Looking back today, my decision in 2001 to head to The Diaspora was life changing. It was a bold move that basically defined my life to date and will continue to do so for many years to come. I rarely thought about the big risk I had taken. While in America, I would recall the fact that I was thousands of miles away from my homeland, but this did not worry me since my fellow immigrants and Americans I knew kept us busy. I established and maintained few friends, though I tend to have advisers in virtually everything I need to know. In terms of contacts, I can be conservative and opportunistic; I still have my high school diaries somewhere in my archives. Heading to The Diaspora was my biggest risk to date but it was a very good decision.

Using a low cost, high value strategy, I managed to get my wife to study in England without any fundraising in Africa. I bought her ticket to England and covered her settlement costs and degree. In Africa, such overseas trips would involve massive fundraising that comes with too many expectations.

When we had our first son, Dylan, in England, my wife was a foreign student. I had just been informed in my job (as Finance and Payroll Assistant) that the organisation would close in about six months due to a failure to win a retendered bid for a major proposal, similar to the one that we had implemented which was core to the organisation. That organisation relied on one large project and the American parent company was not keen to bail the organisation out as theme of intervention was not its strategic priority.

As a foreign student with a limited and short-term visa, I had tough choices to make. Long ago, I had this belief that I would never be illegal in any country. The thought of being jobless with a son to take care of made me quite uncomfortable and unsettled; furthermore, our visas clearly stated that we could not recourse to UK public funds. I knew my wife would not allow me to take radical measures so I planned everything and executed according to my plan; I took action, shared little information, but instead talked in generality. My blue print was a win-win strategy for everyone, however painful it would be.

To make that decision I decided on everyone's role first. For me, my wife's education was top priority, so I told her she will continue with her studies regardless of having an eight-month-old baby boy. For me, I decided to take our son back to Kenya to stay with my mum or mum-in-law, and to me, the priority was to ensure we never used "public funds" in the UK, never mind that I had by then paid lots of money in taxes that I would never possibly claim back. But I had no regrets then since we had learnt a lot by being in Britain.

So my son's future was determined and it was a matter of weeks before he went back to Kenya. For me, I never wanted to hustle looking for jobs with a short-term visa so my only destination was Kenya. I asked my wife to plan her master's studies. Between her first degree and master's there was a gap which would become an elephant immigration question but my wife and I successfully convinced the Home Office (HO). When the HO issue was resolved we felt determined more than ever before, and my wife embarked on to complete her master's studies. It reminded us that our eight-month-old son, who is thirteen years old in 2017, needed to enjoy life free of challenges.

I knew I was departing for abroad in a few weeks and I went crazy with job applications, making applications in the UK, Africa, the Middle East, and around the world. Surprisingly, I got a very cheap flight from the UK to Kenya. My son and I in May 2005 paid GBP 250 for a flight from London Heathrow via Doha to Nairobi.

On landing in Nairobi with my eight-month-old son, he did not want to be babysat by anyone and when he saw me sneaking out, he would scream very loudly and crawl very fast to stop me. My aunties joked that perhaps he was used to the

UK and was wondering why suddenly and overnight people turned black. With all due respect, my auntie said the little boy must be wondering where suddenly some "black monkeys" had dropped from. In a week's time my son had settled and was happy to stay with anyone.

The strategy of low cost, high value was very handy in Nairobi. It was by then exactly four years and three months since I departed Nairobi, Kenya, my homeland, where I had never worked. I managed to live in high income Nairobi West, living off my savings, but this was not to last. In my second week since arriving, on 30 November 2005, I had done several interviews in Nairobi but the most striking one was a phone call from a Dubai-based head-hunter wanting an accountant for a Dubai based international organisation, a private corporation. The many applications for jobs I had made while in Britain had landed me a job. Interestingly, it was a case of a Dubai-based head hunter saying she saw my CV and was keen to shortlist me for the job. I never applied for the job directly but my CV must have been noticed. By end of my second week in Kenya, mid-December 2005, I had already secured an expatriate job in Afghanistan. It was a swift shift of good fortunes.

Since the new employer needed to apply for my Dubai and Afghanistan visa using my Kenya passport, it took a bit long. Finally, I departed for Dubai in January 2006 for a new job to head the finance, administration, and HR unit of a multinational organisation in Dubai but based in Kabul. In Dubai, I was received by employer representative with a big board with my name. The vehicle that picked me was a massive Volvo and I was booked into the guest house for the organization. It was a great feeling.

It was a very interesting moment with myself in Asia, my son in Nairobi, Kenya, and my wife in London, UK. In a record two months a lot of things had moved fast, my journey in The Diaspora continued.

To ensure we meet as a family, I would time my recuperation and rest (R&R) leave and we would meet in Kenya or the UK every three months by alternating the visits. In a way, everyone had retreated to the most ideal environment at that time. I was in Kabul heading key functions of a very extraordinary and dynamic modern corporate organisation; my son would be in Africa with our lovely and large extended family, and my wife would be pursuing her second degree, an MBA, in England. The only separation was distance. With God's grace we had mastered the art of The Diaspora and this journey has compelled me to write about the extraordinary journey we have had, a journey of determination, not fighting with people like the bad side of the modern world, but living tactfully with fullness of joy, regardless of the circumstances of the day. Hope and promise has been our motivator and my best friend; my wife was exceedingly instrumental in this long journey and there is no way I would have made it alone.

The strategy of low cost, high value for money is very powerful and enables one to stay in full control. My American MBA had taught me to be wise. American professors kept encouraging us not to go for yes or no answer in life but always consider "it depends" as the best answer.

The journey in The Diaspora has taught me one thing: that everyone, everything, and every nation matters.

Perception of The Diaspora in host countries

In host countries for The Diaspora, there are always unfounded fears of The Diaspora tearing into existing social and cultural status quo. Apart from isolated cases of a few members of The Diaspora disrupting the social norms in a host country, generally the newly arrived in The Diaspora tend to cautiously fit into the culture of the host countries. The Diaspora rarely bothers about the political situation in host countries, except where immigration policies are not friendly. The social concerns of The Diaspora can drive political concerns in host countries and social concerns tend to be discussed extensively since they have the most conspicuous impact.

The economic impact of The Diaspora tends to be ignored because The Diaspora may constitute a small percentage of the population in host countries.

The most impactful investment of The Diaspora will always remain education since it is a means for significant learning and understanding of how things work in host countries which naturally provides a competitive advantage.

In East Africa, for example, the Arab, Somali, and Indian traders demonstrated a resilient and enduring example of how The Diaspora can hustle, play by the rules, and make a big impact in society. If government policies supported The Diaspora, then the impact of The Diaspora could be rapid and trickle down to the masses.

Regardless of perceptions of The Diaspora in host countries, it is important to be focused and not let isolated sentiments or anti-immigration rhetoric get in one's way; in any case, everyone was once an immigrant—the difference is perhaps who arrived first, and when.

Unfortunately, the nasty face of terrorism has dented The Diaspora, but the good news is that host communities in The Diaspora have well understood that it is only a few who are hell-bent on disrupting societal life, but everyone comes together as always to defeat the sadist terrorists who have no respect for human life, and they belong to hell as we know it. Human life is divine and belongs to God.

First generation of The Diaspora in new world

In advanced economies, the first generation of The Diaspora born in new lands tend to be lucky compared to the immigrant parents, though this depends on the upbringing of the children of immigrants. Quite often, children of new immigrants start life afresh, free from the influence of either the original background of immigrant parents or the new world for immigrant children. Such a start could be positive or negative in a way, hence the crucial role played by the parents. It is for this reason that government policies in host nations matter a lot. Governments that host new immigrants have a big role to play in shaping its destiny as a country. There is often the talk of need for immigrants to fit into new society, an argument that often ignores the extent to which new arrivals are welcome in the first place. The talk is quite often political and too cheap and those who practice the rhetoric may know personally as individuals that such a discussion has no merit; in any case everyone was once an immigrant.

It is always a challenge in The Diaspora to hear all the noise about immigration. Quite frankly, as an individual, it is better to ignore the noises and double hard work and other drivers of success, but ofcourse play by the rules. In any case, Jews provide an enduring example of perseverance. Jews were hated in The Diaspora but they ignored the noises and moved on. The resilience of Joseph in the Bible is what immigrants who mean well and good for the host country need, especially to survive in the long haul.

Human beings easily adapt to new environments. Children especially are the masters of new worlds. Children easily pick up accents and bonds in new worlds quite quickly compared to older generations. This is factual, natural, and beyond human understanding. We are complicated beings, but in a good way. Nature must have allowed children to have a fast footing in The Diaspora as a way to cement bonds. I find it fascinating the way children will know everyone in a neighbourhood much faster than adults.

The way children learn things faster than adults in a new world actually demonstrates what we have always known since time immemorial, that migration has remained divine and will remain the same. The Syria crisis shocked the unprepared world with millions heading for Europe in large numbers, literary on foot, evading well manned gates into the prosperous continent as we know it.

The admissions of millions of refugees, especially in modern Germany, did cause a lot of concern in Europe, but as stated above, immigration, emigration, and The Diaspora have exceeded human imagination throughout history. But despite global migration, it is possible to have peaceful and cohesive societies around the world.

International Aid or The Diaspora

After World War II, the United States set to rebuild the countries of Europe which were devastated by the bloody war. This marked perhaps the first time in human history that a country had developed a strategy to rebuild another one from the rubbles of war. And the Marshall Plan worked very well, far much more that the master planner probably ever imagined.

The success of European countries after World War II accelerated the economic development of the United States. Bilateral trade between the US and EU countries increased.

The master planners of the Marshall Plan knew that a stable world especially Europe was much more guaranteed with capitalism than communism. The Marshall Plan was meant to neutralise communism which had affected much of Europe. The Marshall Plan was therefore a large-scale economic rescue programme. The largest amount of the Marshall Plan, which is over 50% of the funding, was allocated to the UK (26%), France (18%), and West Germany (11%).

Rebuilding after the world war went on beyond Europe, with Asia benefitting as well, even though it was not part of the Marshall Plan.

The United States was founded by immigrants mainly from Europe. The Diaspora of Europe made a pain-staking journey then founded the USA, which years later rescued Europe from the war and provided seed funds that propelled Europe to prosperity.

The Marshall Plan is therefore a historic example where foreign public investments have turned around the economic fortunes of a continent. Most developing countries have been receiving economic aid for almost fifty years, yet economic development has been slow. If international aid does not improve the economic situation for developing countries after the next two decades then something is wrong and the model of economic aid needs to be reviewed to try and understand why it is not working well and how it can work much better; perhaps international aid should focus on high impact and self-sustaining programming.

Aid-giving nations continue to invest tax payers' funds in foreign aid. The good news is aid models have changed in the last decade following difficult and uncomfortable questions being asked. We see a trend of better accountability and value for money initiatives with focus on sustainability.

There is hope that after decades of international aid, things are beginning to work. Most countries in Africa, especially those that have invested in large infrastructure projects, have seen great improvements in recent years.

If governments receiving aid and aid agencies collaborated more closely it could be possible to make use of aid money to increase the impact of aid.

Aid-giving countries need to engage The Diaspora in the setting of priorities for international aid. The Diaspora members could be more knowledgeable in what works best in recipient countries.

The Marshall Plan did work exceedingly well and it is high time impactful interventions are discovered. International aid is taxpayers' money for aid-giving countries and The Diaspora countries make huge sacrifices in order to send the scarce resources abroad. Aid-giving countries need to ensure funds provided in aid either serve the emergency needs or demonstrate an impact in development.

International aid is mentioned herein since it is a subject of interest to all The Diaspora members.

Politics and The Diaspora

However much we ignore politics, it will always be there. Politics and daily life are inseparable and this applies anywhere in the world. One of the reasons for migration into The Diaspora could be political. The Syria crisis for example was caused by political reasons and has had a big impact that has shaped geopolitics in the world.

Unstable political situations continue to make economic and social situations worse, thus increasing the desire for people to move to The Diaspora far away from their homelands. Resolving economic and social issues at their source is one very impactful way of reversing the flight to The Diaspora.

The flight to The Diaspora continues to cause brain drain and brain gain. The people that make it to The Diaspora tend to be the most ambitious, most knowledgeable, and perhaps wealthy. Flight to The Diaspora is a big investment and The Diaspora in a country context could actually mean rural-to-urban migration. We know that across the world more wealth continues to be generated in urban areas compared to rural areas.

Immigration is a zero-sum game. Immigration normally means that there is a brain drain in countries that have emigration and brain gain in countries that have immigration. Even countries that experienced rapid emigration were at a loss for a few years, but once The Diaspora settled and started remittances back to the homeland, the inflows assisted the once deprived countries in stabilising quickly.

The United States, for example, has encouraged a diversity lottery annually and many immigrants made use of the immigration policy to enter the USA. The diversity of the USA remains a national pride and success story even though publicly most White House administrations have admitted the presence of millions of illegal immigrants. It is extremely sad that successive administrations have ignored the importance of legalising the stay of the millions of illegal immigrants.

The Syria crisis was unprecedented and just added to the "to-do" list of complex immigration issues across the world. What started as the Arab Spring resulted in an unprecedented immigration headache for continental Europe; the Arab Spring affected Tunisia, Egypt, Libya, Yemen, Syria, Bahrain, Saudi Arabia, and Morocco. The fall of Muammar Gaddafi made Libya an exit route for immigrants desperate to reach the shores of Europe. Similarly, the fall of Syria led to immigrants from the region literally walking their way with generous Germany admitting over one million people.

For a long time, news was full of information that chaos overseas is easily exported to western fortress countries. Most electorate in Western countries possibly never understood why their governments were spending billions abroad to put out flames. The American administration spoke extensively and repetitively about problems abroad getting exported to the homeland but it is possible the message perhaps never resonated well. The Syria crisis was unprecedented and has demonstrated how the world is interconnected in many ways.

Much as there is politics about The Diaspora, the fact is, The Diaspora will still play an important role in addressing international problems such as that in Syria. The Diaspora remains an important constituent in any country.

89

Impact of The Diaspora in religion

As people migrate into The Diaspora they tend to retain religious beliefs from their country of origin, meaning that The Diaspora can be very beneficial in religious terms. Religion and humanity is inseparable, meaning that The Diaspora will continue to influence religion in the world.

Freedom to religious belief is a right enshrined in nearly all countries of the world, especially dominant religions in each country. On the contrary, some countries around the world have suppressed rights of minority groups to exercise their preferred religions.

The Diaspora continues to be a positive influence in creating religious harmony around the world since The Diaspora export liberal religious mind-sets and not hard-line stances. In a way, The Diaspora is the moderate voice of the world that shapes key issues.

Furthermore, The Diaspora tend to accommodate each other's views and The Diaspora makes an important constituent for many countries around the world. They represent much more open-minded and tolerant constituents especially if the context is volatile.

Impact of The Diaspora changes in charity giving

In western countries, charity giving has accelerated economic development around the world. Some of the most influential international non-governmental organisations (INGOs) continue to play a very important role in humanitarian aid, especially as a source of generous fundraising.

The idea of giving is as old as religion itself. Major religions emphasize charity giving, especially for good causes. The fall in church-going, especially in traditionally religious countries, is a concern, even though The Diaspora has filled the gap but by a very insignificant number.

But the fall in church-going will not reduce charitable giving because gifting is already an embedded culture that will not go away. Charity giving remains a moral imperative and in the UK, for example, the government keeps matching the amount people give for good causes.

Charity fundraisers need to keep up to date with gifting dynamics and constantly staying in touch with givers will go a long way to ensure that charity giving continues as there are plenty of causes to support.

Historically, international aid has made headlines. What is yet to be explored is national fundraising in countries that receive funding. There is need to export the charity giving ideas to countries around the world and try and make it work. We have seen in a lot of countries that Initial Public Offerings

(IPO) by companies selling shares have been oversubscribed, meaning that despite being recipients of international aid, some emerging economies are loaded with money. The yet to happen are targeted efforts to tap on economic prosperity and ensure the well-off assist the struggling lot in these countries - but there is emergence of southern based development organisations which are doing well.

In Kenya, the success of mobile money transfer has made fundraising efforts very easy, faster than anywhere else in the world. Within a few minutes, it is becoming increasingly possible to mobilise fundraising on a great scale.

Charity giving for good causes needs to be encouraged in The Diaspora. The needs in aid-receiving countries will continue to increase due to ever-emerging emergencies as well as a big shortfall in development funding. The Diaspora can play an important role in addressing long-term development as well as development in the aftermath of emergency situations.

The unfounded pitfalls in The Diaspora

Departing the comforts of home into The Diaspora can be an exciting journey with risks and opportunities in equal measure. The Diaspora in itself is a great adventure that is not regrettable. There is so much to learn in The Diaspora but initially there are anxious moments, especially when one is new in The Diaspora.

Pitfalls in The Diaspora kick in when fears and risks materialise. The things that lead to pitfalls include sickness, loss of job, accident, fighting, breach of laws, excessive debts, theft, relationship issues, loss of home, overstaying visas and work permits, problem getting visas and work permits, loss of family members anywhere in the world, and other reasons. In The Diaspora, rather than focus on pitfalls, it is better to remain positive and work out a winning strategy, and this book aims to inspire people to succeed in The Diaspora.

I have been very fortunate in The Diaspora with God's help to have avoided nearly all the pitfalls except inevitable ones such as loss of family members back in the country of origin.

Success in The Diaspora is driven by a positive mind-set or attitude, patience, confidence, hope, faith, belief in God, discipline, hard work, adherence to law, timeliness, stability of family, avoidance of regressive beliefs, and teamwork. Avoiding failure in The Diaspora is possible if one at least works towards what drives success in The Diaspora. There is always a misconception that one has to have lots of money in

The Diaspora which is not true. What normally counts is good planning, being organised, making the right decisions, and having the virtues described below.

Positive mind-set or attitude is perhaps the most powerful virtue one can have. When I departed Africa for my master's studies in America, I was driven largely by aspirations, hope, and good outlook of the world, rather than fears that have denied humanity the chance to enjoy life. The people who first hosted me in America were an American family I had identified online, and I paid for my stay until I left after identifying college mates in my first few weeks in Oklahoma City. My first roommate in America was an African immigrant who had left Tanzania for Europe several years ago. He was married, with two girls who lived in Europe.

When I arrived in America, I had saved enough money from my expatriate job in Hargeisa, Somaliland, therefore I was able to survive in America for at least eight months without a job. And to complicate matters, I had just left my current wife, then-girlfriend, in Africa. Equally, I had left countless family members and relatives in Africa. Of course, I would later play a good role in uplifting some of our siblings even while I was struggling as an MBA student in America.

I was quite lucky to have bought a vehicle in Oklahoma City which I used for almost nine months. I was so busy with life that I forgot to change the car oil or top up the oil. I remember one morning I was driving at almost eighty miles per hour on an interstate road in Oklahoma City when my car had a loud smoky burst and the car suddenly smoked heavily. I managed to stop the car safely and ordered my friends, to whom I gave a ride to university, to embark safely. That day we hired a taxi to take us to university where we attended the lectures of the day.

In the meantime, I had arranged for a mechanic to tow my car to the garage. I later found out that the car was a write-off. I searched for a replacement car shortly afterwards and got one. Since then I have been quite careful with oil changes in vehicles and ensuring timely service of cars.

Even in times of challenge and despair, my determination and attitude remained intact. In The Diaspora, one will encounter endless challenges just like anywhere else but what makes a difference is how you emerge successfully from the problem of the day, and positive mind-set is a winning attribute.

Patience was my real challenge in life. I could be very impatient, especially where time was concerned. To date, inefficiency and lack of effectiveness rattle me badly and usually I would not fear to register my impatience where efficiency and effectiveness were in jeopardy.

My greatest test for my patience was my then-girlfriend (now wife); I knew her in 1999. After knowing her, we became great friends and even though I had great confidence in her, I never had the fear that we will not meet again and went ahead to America, leaving her behind. Though I was optimistic we would meet someday, I knew the journey would be long. She left Kenya for England in January 2003 and I would join her in October 2003 straight from the USA. We finally reunited in the UK after two years. On 11 September 2004 we had a private wedding and our firstborn, Dylan, was born in November 2004. For an extremely impatient person, two years was far too long but we pulled through with my current wife, mother of three boys. The Diaspora requires a lot of patience since things may not work out that easily. Many things can stand in one's way and lack of patience can make one miss out on opportunities.

Confidence is something to earn over time and The Diaspora requires exceptional confidence not just the basic confidence. I did improve by confidence over time through the learning process since the lack of knowledge is the big reason for weak confidence. My humble beginnings in Kenya quite often tested my confidence. I gained much confidence progressively in life which is quite normal. My first job after university in 1999 was an expatriate job and ever since I have lived outside my country of birth. Survival would have been impossible if I lacked confidence, since outside the comfort zone what one needs the most is the confidence and self-determination to go through the endless challenges of life. Confidence has given me much determination in life and one of the key drivers to write this book is to share my journey in The Diaspora with the hope of inspiring more people to have full and unwavering confidence as they face challenges, especially in The Diaspora.

Unfortunately, a lack of confidence can be easily noticeable in, say, job interviews. Building confidence is not a matter of having a brave face, but understanding pertinent issues in a situation. Knowledge is power and one way to build confidence is to gather exceptional knowledge.

In a military context, confidence counts and in modern warfare winning a war can sometimes mean winning confidence first. In famous football, confidence matters a lot. If one does homework well before any major event or appointment, then confidence is guaranteed and we know success and confidence go together.

Hope, faith, and belief in God—I truly believe in the next world. While adventuring abroad I have had hope, faith, and

96

belief in God which have been extremely private in nature. Even in church, while other believers speak in tongues as they say, I would stay composed but with hope, faith, and belief in God. I believe in God's word, that I could dare to take an oath and swear about it.

I believe that God created every one equal and in His image and what possibly differentiates human beings is the product of stains in human life which would not exist in God's presence. If there is something I have done correctly in life it is the hope, faith, and belief I have in God. In a secular world, the norm may dictate that we do not show faith publicly, but I strongly believe this weakens our society, especially societies that had strong religious beginnings. I am willing to lose everything in life but the hope, faith, and belief in God are paramount, especially in The Diaspora. The Bible is the most important book, especially to the Christians, and is different from all other books as it defines humanity right from the beginning to the next world.

Discipline and hard work. In The Diaspora, a combination of discipline and hard work can make one do and achieve quite a lot. The only studies that involved attending full-time classes were my undergraduate and master's degrees, and this could be because these degrees normally require some percentage of attendance; normally seventy per cent is the expected attendance. I remember in my undergraduate degree in the University of Nairobi, I would score high grades with limited attendance to lectures, which made me at odds with my university professors, especially geography professors, who were then widely travelled globally.

My geography classes in the University of Nairobi were exciting since I had university professors who had travelled the globe, and apparently had different types of eye glasses to suit driving, lectures, reading, and international conferences. Some would put on up to three specs or glasses by the time the lecture ended. I recall one time in a packed lecture hall I became so impatient with a lecturer taking the first half an hour talking about personal adventures and trips abroad that I became rattled and walked away from the packed lecture hall as I had other engagements. That remained my regret in university lecture halls but I consoled myself with the fact that I had important engagements such as work and other private studies to do. Later that evening my colleagues described the awkward moment I walked away from packed the lecture hall as awkward, but too brave and confident.

Success in The Diaspora requires discipline and hard work and the two remain intertwined. I have done lots of studies via distance and online studies and two virtues that guarantee success in such a scenario remain discipline and hard work. Discipline may have many definitions as you may find out online or via dictionaries, but the discipline I am talking about involves setting winning strategies and objectives and backing them up with a robust action plan.

Equally, the meaning and context of hard work may vary but the one I am referring to is the hard work that ensures that discipline is consistent, habitual, and sustainable. A habit is a behaviour that is consistently repeated and is thus sustainable. It is therefore correct to say that discipline and hard work remain the most powerful combination of virtues that guarantee success in The Diaspora.

Adherence to law is perhaps the most important thing to do, especially outside the comfort zone or normal environment. In advanced countries, adherence to law is the only hope for success since in these environments it is not possible to buy one's way out of law. Rule of law is perhaps the most important virtue that makes advanced nations successful and above all others. The Diaspora tends to have a lot of strict laws which must be obeyed and anyone from jurisdictions that do not observe rule of law may find it hard to survive in The Diaspora.

Timeliness is perhaps one of the most important things to observe in The Diaspora, even when timeliness is not necessarily a habitual preference culturally. When one is new in The Diaspora, as frequently happens to most immigrants, time is a priority and important.

Immigration laws may change quite quickly in The Diaspora countries, and timeliness is an important attribute to try and keep in touch with changing regulations. To make it worse, the State has no obligation to update immigrants on changing immigration laws and practices. And ignorance of the law, including timeliness, is not a defence

Stable family is a major motivator for immigrants who have made a choice about family life. But even those without family of their own still rely on fellow The Diaspora for support. Lack of stable family in The Diaspora is difficult, since the newly arrived may well lack experienced people to provide useful advice. To me, family has been the greatest motivator: when I endure extremely cold weather to walk into train stations to commute to work, the family is in mind; when I endure high temperatures to get to work, the family is equally in mind. Family is everything and a stable one is a great blessing.

It is amazing how The Diaspora changes priorities for parents. Children born in The Diaspora command their own way of life that is very distinct from that of the immigrant parents, yet there is continuous learning from both experiences, that of adults and children in new world—they are experiences that are extremely complementary to each other. There may be occasional clashes in culture but these can be talked through in amicable ways, with due respect.

An unstable family is very demanding and perhaps more demanding than life in The Diaspora. It is therefore self-defeating when members of The Diaspora start having family breakdowns. Members of The Diaspora ought to understand that having family breakdowns in The Diaspora is a futile exercise. No relationship is easy and members of The Diaspora are encouraged to try, in the long haul, to stay in peace and harmony unless irrevocably red lines are crossed.

Avoidance of regressive beliefs. The Diaspora is a big opportunity for The Diasporas and addressing bottlenecks is a major step to success in The Diaspora. While in The Diaspora in the US and UK, I realised that some members of The Diaspora believed that some achievements are impossible or are consigned to a particular group of people. But as a matter of fact, great achievements in The Diaspora lie squarely on self-belief that defies expectations and usual norms. One must be willing to think outside the box and away from the comfort zone. There is no need to believe in some upper ceiling created for some, but strive to overcome barriers which do exist everywhere one goes, not just in The Diaspora.

Failure to believe in oneself makes things hard and deters efforts to change the status quo and misconceptions. God created everyone equally, male and female, man and woman, in his own image, and whatever exists as a barrier is man-made.

Teamwork refers to the combined efforts of a group working towards the same goals. Efficiency and effectiveness remain the most important barometers of teamwork, and success in The Diaspora, in all spheres, quite often depends on how one is not only seen to be a team player but demonstrates evidence of solid teamwork. It takes some effort to build the rapport of a diverse workforce.

Teamwork promotes better ways of working with cross-learning. Work is usually interdependent and this makes teamwork a big factor in recruitment in The Diaspora. There is no interview one will ever attend and miss emphasis about teamwork. The slightest indicator of a person who values no teamwork is an automatic disqualification.

Healthy living in The Diaspora

There is so much to gain from The Diaspora. It can be a journey of endless gains but can also be a big elephant. Big gains can be made socially and economically. Socially, one has the opportunity to interact with people from many countries which makes one easily adapt into any culture. Economically, gains are massive, but only if one is lucky enough to gain full and unrestricted rights and obligations in The Diaspora. Social and economic well-being, as elaborated, have a direct impact on well-being and healthy living.

The scope of this book is not to prescribe healthy living and well-being, but to provide a few tips based on real life experience. In particular, I will try and describe choices for healthy living and how it varies from the homeland into The Diaspora. Particular emphasis will be put on how success in life can lead to unintentional deterioration in healthy living, and this will focus on the extremely well-off in society with less knowledge about healthy living. Success in life may lead one to a lifestyle that does not promote healthy living; for example, success derived from endless hustling and a stressful life can easily trigger health problems. Equally, success in life that leads to a passive life and unhealthy eating can create health problems.

In my journey in The Diaspora I have come across different cultures with different sensitivity to healthy living. I will start from my native Kenya. I was brought up in the Great Rift Valley (GRV) of Kenya, and the GRV is the food basket of Kenya with a diverse climate of all extremes. The GRV perhaps only lacks the freezing winters of the northern hemisphere to complete all the types of climates on Earth. I was thus gifted with plenty of food and my parents never knew what drought was. What we used to call drought in the good days were reduced harvests, which are technically not droughts.

In my native Kenya, healthy living was about adequate food to eat and never becoming sick, and the two indicators of plenty of food and no sickness were misconstrued to mean healthy living, which is not correct. In fact, eating *Ugali* and *Nyama Choma*, trademark food in Kenya, is considered a sign of success and wealth. This fallacy of eating meat daily is still a practice in many countries around the world.

In the capital, Nairobi, I lived with my brothers, sometimes sisters and other relatives, and the diet was quite good and diverse and not like the predictable diets in rural Kenya. Fruits and vegetables increased in variety and the menu was more complicated than in rural Kenya. When I moved to the capital, Nairobi, in 1994, I must admit the transition was a bit odd to me. Food servings was normally a buffet, the self-serving were small but double the ones I had in high school boarding, but the quantity could not match the sizeable standard portions made in rural Kenya, especially the GRV. In rural areas, I could serve as many plates as I could, but quite frankly I usually did one and a half servings maximum, that is, serve a full plate, then going for half before completing my food.

In the capital, Nairobi, the culture was a first serving only from the buffet and most people rarely thought of an additional half serving. Well, I tried both depending on the meal of the day and my brother was extremely generous, perhaps the most generous person I have ever lived with apart from my mum and my wife. Interestingly, the subject of healthy eating and healthy living never clicked still; it was not in my agenda despite seeing my brother head for the gym. Social media and the internet were still being manufactured in the Silicon Valley.

My brother was extremely lucky. He would take us out every weekend for drinks and fun and paid the bills, he was very generous. I am yet to meet such a man in my life even after globe-trotting four continents of the world. He played a key role in my journey into The Diaspora and this book is also a dedication to the key role he played in shaping me and many of my brothers, sisters, cousins, and relatives in the wider family. I left my brother's house in Nairobi to take up my first assignment in The Diaspora, in Hargeisa, Somaliland. In Somaliland, as described elsewhere in this book, I lived a kingly life with everything I needed. I missed the food in my brother's house in Nairobi. I ended up leaving Hargeisa in 2001 very clueless about healthy living. But Somaliland was a good context. Somalia is dry and the food available is very healthy. Meat was either chicken or beef but I found the food heathy, though eating meat daily was a cultural practice. Fruits were not plenty but we had enough vegetables to make up for the lack of fruits.

My next destination was the USA where food changed completely. Food was of a different variety and there were plenty of eateries. We had lots of fun with food and tried virtually every food we could think of. Food rations in the USA are massive and eating in the USA is a very social event full of fun. At work, American colleagues brought lots of food and it was a vibrant culture, very nice. I still missed food in my native Kenya. The portions in the USA matched that prepared by my Mum in rural Kenya but were rich in diversity to that in my prior locations in The Diaspora. The variety of food in the USA, though in excess of what I had before, actually made me remember quite often the food in my brother's house in Nairobi. To break away from eating out, a trademark of American living, I occasionally cooked the Kenyan *Ugali* which was quite surprising as it cooked very quickly on gas, which I wondered if it was of better quality I had seen before.

Like in any advanced nation, gas was readily available, which was nice as I had not much time to cook. I left America clueless about healthy eating. Indeed, my mission to America was to study, adventure, and have fun, and healthy eating never bothered me. My life then was like my Fridays now: days where I permit myself to eat any food outside of a strict healthy diet.

From America, I went to the UK and met my wife, girlfriend then. She loved to cook Kenyan food as she is from Kenya originally, like me. Food in England is very diverse and you get any food in plenty just like the ones available anywhere else in the world. We are fond of homemade food and many times I offer my wife money to buy ready-food from outside but instead, she prefers to cook and she never gets tired of it, bless her. I left the UK for abroad in November 2005 and ended up in Afghanistan in January 2006 and stayed until August 2007 before heading back to the UK.

In Kabul, the capital city of Afghanistan, I had the best food in the world, though missed fresh fish in the UK. One of the business units for my employer, a multinational conglomerate, was a catering unit providing catering services to multinational military forces and commercial flights. I was head of the finance, administration, and HR function that delivered the catering services to the military of the free world. The job was historic and so was the eating. We had several chefs that came from countries that have some of the best chefs in the world especially India, Bangladesh, Nepal, and Pakistan. It was a five-star hotel type of food for every meal from breakfast to late night, if anyone had the appetite to eat.

On a daily basis, our cleaners would replenish fresh drinks in small fridges in our self-contained rooms. But we worked very hard and deserved the best treatment. Serving the military of the free world was not easy. I left Afghanistan in August 2007 clueless about healthy living. I had put on some weight but perhaps due to long working hours and little activity. We once asked for a gym and our kind employer provided one but we were just too busy for a boring gym and lacked the mob psychology to motivate each other to go to the gym. Life was good and I love to have made history serving the military of the free world via private contracting at a critical time in history.

From Afghanistan, I went back to England in August 2007 but I was still clueless about healthy living even though I started being a bit conscious, but mainly because of publicly available information from the internet on healthy living. I remember ignoring several reminders for routine medical checks. I was perhaps copying my dad in Africa who would see the doctor only when sick and not for routine medical checks which he considered a waste of time; indeed, back in Africa, people would carry on for decades without going for routine medical checks.

I have since discovered that actually the people who needed no routine check-up yet lived quite long were several generations before us who never saw the modern world and the artificial foods of our modern age. Their world was naturally organic, far from the artificial foods and exotic life of the modern age.

After a certain age in major advanced countries, routine medical checks are carried out in what people refer to as human "MOT". MOT stands for Ministry of Transport and annually in UK, vehicles undergo mandatory and extremely thorough vehicle inspection and emission testing, a practice I am yet to see another country that does it that thoroughly. In the past, I did medical checks but only for work or education-related reasons, not as part of routine health checks. I finally obliged and went for routine medical checks which were all right but just like vehicle MOT had some interesting advisories; for sure advances in medicine have made life better. The health check showed I was perhaps too passive and I needed to be exercising in addition to working on few things that are necessary for healthy living. It was a shock, since by any standard I was not obese. Perhaps I had a small pot belly, due to my weekend six-pack, which would make me disappointed if a doctor ever recommends cutting me off six-pack entirely. However, as part of healthy living, I chose to downgrade from six-pack to four-pack strictly on weekends (Fridays and or Saturdays) but perhaps with top ups of better substance, otherwise how can one deal with weekends; I believe staying healthy does not mean we deprive ourselves the little pleasures in life in any case some already claim life is too short for too much discipline. Actually, in the course of The Diaspora life, I have found many people who seem either negligent or innocent about health issues like excessive weight. But I was extremely pleased to have gone against upbringing norm and opted for routine medical checks, a practice that makes me feel like a teenager in age. Had I opted to continue with old way of life of not bothering about healthy living, it would have possibly caught up with me.

It will be great injustice for healthy living if I do not describe what pot belly means in different culture. While living in Africa, pot belly was considered a sign of well-being and a trademark for possessing lots of money. But as we know it now, pot belly comes with health issues that could progress in the wrong direction if not addressed on time. I though readers of this book should know this information on pot belly just for information and action.

Due to upbringing, really, I did not care so much about healthy living; but it was more of a lack of knowledge rather than being careless. The purpose of this book is not only to document my life story but to share it so that readers can benefit. One such benefit is on healthy living and I will explain what I have known in layman's terms. I could become anything in the world but a doctor. At a young age, I could not even slaughter a goat, let alone cut the head of a headless chicken, so being a doctor never crossed my mind. But medical professionals are important people in our lives; they work tirelessly to keep us healthy.

So **what is healthy living, especially in The Diaspora?** From my experience in The Diaspora, healthy living means eating well, avoiding bad eating, avoiding stress, maintaining good relationships with people, exercising, and going for routine medical checks.

Eating well means the body gets all the nutrients it needs. Avoiding stress means our bodies are safe from generating free radicals which tamper badly with body mechanisms. Bad eating must be avoided and bad eating involves taking more food components than the body requires. Excessive fats, salt, and carbohydrates are the silent killers of our modern time.

Avoiding stress is very important as this can lead to many health problems. Stress accelerates free radicals which damage body cells and cause many other problems. Stress causes the body to function excessively, which means body organs overwork themselves.

Maintaining good relationships with people has the opposite impact of the consequences of stress. Good relationships nurture the body. Just think of the smile of a little infant, how it makes you smile—that is what good relationships do, and they relax the body, meaning there is no chance for toxic chemicals to be produced.

Exercise is good and in The Diaspora, thorough exercise burns excess weight and refreshes the body, meaning that after good exercise, one can have a good night's sleep like a baby; that good sleep and plenty of it rejuvenates the body.

Routine medical checks are good and should not look like a pass or fail in an exam. They are done to ensure that healthy living indictors are intact; if the indicators are abnormal, they provide a chance for corrective action to be done before it is too late.

As stated above, excessive fats, salt, and carbohydrates are the silent killers of our modern time. Excessive fats can find their way into the blood steam and could affect the flow of blood and damage blood vessels. Basically, they affect blood vessels in sensitive parts of the body and this happens with age.

Excessive salt is as bad as excessive fats. In layman's language, it is as if the excessive salt crystallises, thus blocking the seamless flow of vital ingredients the body needs.

Excessive carbohydrates are the least known "time bomb" of our modern time. Carbohydrates, in a nutshell, provide energy to the body, and there is a sophisticated process that converts the starch into energy in the form of sugar. Not everyone utilises carbohydrates in the same way; everyone on earth is different. Some people may find excess glucose is not mopped up by the body, thus creating excess sugar in the body. Food is like a pipe of water. If you open it slightly, less flows out, and if you open a tap fully, the flow can be disastrous. Our body works that way: everything you take in has to come out through a process, so quite frankly, the less, the better. Repeated research had shown that people who eat less live longer. Imagine our body organs still function since we came to this world as babies and it does so 24/7 without complaining.

As a father, I was impressed by the process of getting children in the UK. I was lucky to be in the delivery room for my first- and third-born. I missed our second-born since I had to babysit whilst we awaited the arrival of the baby. The second-born was born while the first-born and I were asleep. I had slept a few hours earlier, and upon waking up, he was already born. My mobile also had fifteen missed calls and it was my wife calling me that the process was underway.

Unfortunately, the long wait and part-time taking care of our big son had made me miss the arrival of the second-born.

As you can imagine, right from birth, our bodies self-sustain and do so through a mix of dynamics. In fact, the human body is very strong indeed and a proper mix of food, exercise, and generally healthy living enables us to exist for the long haul.

Quite often on Facebook I see people deem relationships as "complicated". Perhaps the little-known complication in our lives is the health aspect of it. It remains complicated, yet the messaging about healthy living is very difficult to disseminate. As you can see, it took my journey in four continents to understand the basics that not all doctors can explain in details or have the time to explain. Nurses just do routine checks with some explanations, and normally it is up to one's doctor to explain medically what goes on. Nutritionists are just like the dentists, perhaps a preserve of the elite class in some countries due to need and cost concerns. Therefore, it can be very hard to get the services of nutritionists to explain some of the things that matter in healthy living. We remember the days of being told too much taking of eggs is dangerous and then, a few months down the line, we are told again that too many eggs is not harmful.

In fact, most doctors prefer not to disappoint people and quite often may avoid going into much details. But actually, once a person is enlightened it becomes easy to understand the doctor. If anything, once you understand the mechanics of healthy living, it makes it easy to engage medical professionals in conversations. Healthy living therefore remains a less understood subject and is taken less seriously since a shift away from healthy living may involve painful choices that few dare to implement; imagine being told to discontinue your favourite food, drinks, and lifestyle and, to make it worse, being asked to do more exercise. We have had stories of people being told for example to stop drinking and smoking, but out of frustration they end up drinking and smoking even more—as if in protest.

The biggest tip in healthy living is perhaps the small print which many of us avoid while shopping. In most food stuffs, the small print comes in the form of colours, with red being the thing to avoid, orange being things to take in moderation and otherwise better to avoid, and green being okay to consume. In some advanced countries, this has been called "wheel of health". Ever since I got enlightened, I have been shopping using colour codes and unless it is a Friday and/or Saturday, my two days of indulgence, I try and avoid red colour coded food and go for moderation in orange and embrace green.

But the green colour code must be taken too in moderation because every food has starch of different measures and a healthy food taken excessively may create other issues.

Eating in moderation is the secret to good health in The Diaspora and cultural norms ought to be challenged. In some communities in Africa and other continents, eating meat daily is a sign of wealth but actually, in actual fact, it can be a license to an early grave. Every country has staple foods. In West Africa it is yams, in Asia it is rice, and in East and Southern Africa it is *Ugali*. Staple food tends to be taken in large bulk as it is a cultural norm. I remember in the good old days I would eat big *Ugali*, plenty of *sukuma wiki*, and then follow that with full cream milk. It took me very long to figure out that the diet was not as good as I used to assume. The quantity eaten by then was shocking and it is a miracle people have not got sick though increasingly lifestyle diseases are shifting to emerging in developing countries. There is an urgent need to adopt heathy lifestyles; in any case, unhealthy living is putting much pressure on the scarce resources on the planet. The Diaspora, to me, has been more than a journey; it was a whole life lived and hence, the reason of wanting to write this book as a living testimony, to build a very compelling case of major issues in our life.

For more information on healthy living I encourage you to start a conversation with your health professionals. Feel at liberty to challenge any of the aforementioned experiences. You are free to either agree or disagree but I hope you will find the information very useful.

Food colour code is shown below (*kindle version shows colour; Paperback version is black and white*). The example was obtained from the National Health Service UK website:

Slide 4 - Healthy eating in diaspora matters
Narrative below by Hillary Rono @ Life in The Diaspora

In The Diaspora, one ignores **will of health** at own peril. Eating much more than the body needs is a habit I have personally observed as damaging in diaspora. Personally, it took me time to get the facts. Since knowing the meaning of colour code of food, I shop very cautiously and look at will of health for every food purchase I make. **Energy** is the capacity to work and our body runs on energy basically. So the intake of energy depends on body metabolism and level of activity. If one is passive in life, then less energy is needed. Energy is rarely colour coded but calories are shown. **Fats and saturates** are usually colour coded, advise is to stick to amber in small quantity and modestly in green. **Sugar** which is red in colour is unhealthy and must be avoided. I take sugary stuff only on special occasions such as birthday, valentine and Christmas and avoid it all the other time. **Salt** is always colour coded depending on the quantity involved. **Colour code below from NHS England website.**

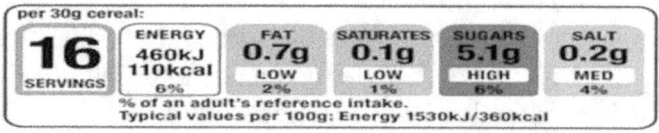

As an assignment, I leave you, my esteemed reader, to research on what constitutes bad fats and good fats. **Slide 4**

above shows fats in green. Saturates are fats too. Please research on good fats and talk to your health professionals about it.

Do have a healthy life, dear esteemed reader.

The complications of relocating from The Diaspora.

My journey to The Diaspora was perhaps the cheapest and easiest. Before I wrote my final exams in the University of Nairobi in September 1999, I had already secured my first job in The Diaspora as an expat. My employer therefore paid all my bills in The Diaspora and what I only needed to worry about was to deliver, and I am sure I did. With a large residence, protected by six guards and an almost fortress-like office and accommodation complex, I had no reason not to deliver. We established the first microfinance institution in Hargeisa, Somaliland, that lent money to Somaliland nationals, and we followed the principles of Sharia law and this made my first job delicate culturally.

It is while in Hargeisa, Somaliland, that I secretly planned my journey to The Diaspora in America. In fact, it was so secretive that not even my then-employer knew my intentions, but after two years in Somaliland it was time to do something else and the desire to pursue MBA degree studies enticed me to arrive at what to do next.

Before relocating back from The Diaspora, one needs to plan very well and where possible, get something running before making a final sign off. Over time, things change and indeed things would have changed since one left their original country. There is a story of a Kenyan national who left Kenya decades past when perhaps we had a very simple airport terminal in Nairobi's Jomo Kenyatta International Airport

113

(JKIA). Upon their return in recent years, I understand the returnee asked whether he had landed at the right airport; perhaps he thought he had landed in an American city. Decades later, his native country, Kenya, had moved on, despite political bickering which seems to happen every election time. Just like the pain-staking journey of leaving for The Diaspora, returning to the original homeland equally needs meticulous planning.

For countries struggling with immigration issues, I think there are solutions out there. With enough resources, global migration can be rebalanced but it needs the stamina of the founders of the Marshall Plan after World War II.

Relocating back from The Diaspora is always difficult, especially after a long period of stay. The reasons to relocate are discussed below and include improving economic and political situations, an end of The Diaspora mission, to take a new job abroad, to manage foreign investments abroad, limited opportunities in The Diaspora, death of a family members, aging parents, change of The Diaspora country, and other factors.

Improving economic situation. For The Diaspora that were taken into exile by difficult economy back in the country of origin, improving economic situations can always entice members of The Diaspora back into their original homeland, the comfort zone. But even when economic situations are improving, there is always no guarantee that at a personal level, things will work easily.

The business environment is competitive and we know that in developing countries, business competition and rivalry can lead to bad consequences. The Diaspora members seeking this route need to first "test the waters"; that is, ensure the business idea works before packing for good since packing back to The Diaspora can be a very painful exercise, as some may have noticed, especially if the attempt to relocate backfires or hits a brick wall.

Improved political situation. Some members of The Diaspora may have gone into self or forced exile in The Diaspora because of limited political space. The 2017 protracted election in Kenya is a reminder that political situations can be fluid. Kenya's political turbulence peaked in the 1990s with agitation of the multi-party political system. Kenya has had a very stable political climate compared to other countries in Africa and beyond, but Kenya's case is interesting because the political situation seemed progressive and stable. I am not implying that it has been regressive sometimes, but after the 2007 post-election violence (PEV), it is no longer easy to take things for granted. Kenya has progressed well, especially since the first unified political group took over power in 2002 after many years of being run by a single political party establishment.

This year, 2017, marked fifteen years since the change in leadership and demonstrates good progress in a short period of time, though recent political developments are worrying. For The Diaspora formerly exiled by political situations, it remains clear that returning back from exile requires one to exercise caution since politics in developing and emerging countries can be turbulent. We have seen similar situations in some of the Asian countries. The Arab Spring in the Middle East did give false hope and it remains to be seen what the ultimate result will be for the hard fought agitation for change in governance. It is likely that The Diaspora members from emerging and developing countries will monitor democratic developments

115

before deciding to go back to the original homeland for good, in case returning back is on the cards.

End of The Diaspora mission. One of the easiest excuses to return to the original homeland for good remains the end of the mission in The Diaspora. Many have followed this route. When I graduated from Oklahoma City University with an MBA in May 2003, I was reluctant to return back to Kenya because of the fluid economic situation. By contrast, my fellow university mates from China were doing exactly the opposite— they would graduate on a Friday afternoon and on a Monday, two days later, they would be on government chartered flights back to mainland China. The Chinese government has invested massively in the education of its citizens and as global students, we know the things that have made China such a successful country. Most of my university mates in the MBA class already had good jobs awaiting them in China. An end of the mission in The Diaspora such as education, college, exchange visit, or ordinary short visit normally marks the end of the road in The Diaspora.

Taking a job abroad is usually one of the key and perhaps the sweetest reasons for being in The Diaspora. Taking a new job abroad remains the best excuse for one to return to their original homeland after a period of time in The Diaspora. But relocating back to the original homeland after a period of time in The Diaspora needs to be considered carefully. So many factors that matter in life come into consideration when making such a move.

Managing foreign investments abroad usually becomes an enticement to return to original homeland. Many members of The Diaspora have suffered immensely due to a misuse of their hard-earned money by fund managers abroad. There are

116

situations where The Diaspora have remitted funds abroad only to find out that nothing has been done, yet all the money is gone. This remains a big hypocrisy by those corrupting hard-earned funds by The Diaspora.

Unfortunately, it becomes very hard to enforce such agreements because in most cases, it constitutes a gentleman's agreement which may not be enforceable. Furthermore, those involved could be blood relatives, thus making prosecution difficult because in most cultures, especially African, it is a taboo to sue one's own relative, let alone a brother or sister. Members of The Diaspora are usually left with the option of either returning back to their homeland or disposing of the investments. Disposing could be a painful experience since some of the assets were bought for low prices and disposing them really means it will never be possible to afford such assets again and such a step can be an awfully regressive move. The only option sometimes is to return back to the original homeland to manage assets and investments with the hope that the income from the assets would exceed income one would comfortably earn abroad. It needs a serious trade-off and it can be a zero-sum game of losing in one place and making it back from another.

Limited opportunities in The Diaspora can sometimes force members of The Diaspora to return to their original homeland. There are so many barriers out there and it is not easy to overcome barriers. Sometimes progressing may mean tactical or permanent and strategic relocation from The Diaspora.

I have in the past tactically relocated to The Diaspora in other countries and seen it to be of much help after returning back; this is equivalent to cultural exchange visits where

117

participants learn a lot from a different setting, far away from the comforts of home. Such a move comes with risks but The Diaspora is a group of people with a risk appetite already, so relocations should not be a big deal, instead it looks like taking a bus to some new villages somewhere in the middle of nowhere.

Death of a family member is always quite devastating when it happens. I stopped counting the number of families who passed on while I was abroad. This is usually difficult and for me, my consolation has been the fact that there is nothing I could do as an individual to prevent or delay some things but at many times I have had to contribute to cover costs or make a phone call to console. Unless it is a very close family member the fact is one cannot afford to board a plane for each and every passing on of a relative. Those affected have been very understanding, which is much appreciated. Death is a reality in life and the cruel hand is usually untimely. Most members of The Diaspora attend farewells, then head back to The Diaspora whenever the unfortunate happens. Normally it is a very expensive undertaking that comes without any notice.

Worldwide, The Diaspora have faced the cruel hand of death and it is always good for The Diaspora to take insurance to guard against unforeseen events. Unfortunately such insurance covers only the immediate family and most of the insurance normally excludes children. But all adults in The Diaspora need to take life insurance which can be cheap since chances of unfortunate happenings are usually remote and insurance companies do make a lot of money over the years from exceptionally low or scarce insurance claims.

The Diaspora need to learn to transfer risks and insurance is the best way of transferring risks. The Diaspora people have

118

got a risk appetite but that should not mean that risks are taken blindly.

Aging parents remain a very challenging situation. The Diasporas support parents quite a lot and there is no joy as good as knowing that parents are happy and healthy. For me, I cannot count how many times just calling my parents while in The Diaspora made me quite happy, exceedingly happy. As parents age, health concerns take a toll, and this happens everywhere, not just in The Diaspora. The only difference is that in The Diaspora, parents may be thousands of miles away. It is common for The Diaspora to leave work or even relocate so as to take care of parents. Such moral support to parents is quite important.

At some point in life we all age and taking care of aging parents is one way for The Diaspora to show love and pass the same to children. Taking care of aging parents ought to be the culture and norm of any society. In The Diaspora, I have heard adults who have already had the conversations with children and already made a wish for preferred future care. The majority of the people prefer home care which is the ancient and quite old preferred practice of caring for aging parents.

The world has changed though with children getting increasingly busy with less time in disposal to undertake home care. Aging parents keep getting fewer choices for care and the most preferred option could be the most expensive and least affordable.

Change of The Diaspora country is sometimes necessary for work or business. I have been lucky to work in America, Europe, Asia and the Middle East, and in African countries outside my country of birth. Changing country is sometimes inevitable since life is indeed a long journey of risks, adventures, and challenges.

Sometimes it becomes necessary to change The Diaspora country and people should not shy away from taking the bold step of changing country, especially where it makes life easy and prospects better even if as a tactical move. I find it strange when The Diaspora give up on good opportunities abroad but they do miss the fun. The same member of The Diaspora may complain endlessly about stagnation in career and other things that matter in life but then decline to take offers abroad. Described below is some of my adventure in The Diaspora; when one is busy in The Diaspora, time moves very fast.

Working in America is quite nice. I remember lots of dinners and lunches I had with Americans. There is lots of food in America and plenty of eating places. There are quite a lot of food drive-through. It was fascinating for American professors in business school to buy food for the entire class on special occasions. In all my academic and professional studies, I found that moment to be the most exciting and I still recall it very well in 2017, fourteen years after it happened.

I loved the very close interactions with the African-Americans, especially the ladies; they would not shy away from expressing their feelings and opinions openly; they were not like the measured and little-exposed ladies in rural Africa or perhaps other parts of the world, even though modern social media has almost enlightened everyone. Even pensioners in rural Africa are on Facebook!

Weekends in USA were fascinating. Gas stations for fuelling cars, as they call it in America, are usually packed on weekends as people gas vehicles to drive about and around.

Given another chance in life, I would not mind to live in America, though it is far from my original homeland in Kenya but much nearer to lovely Britain, the best place I have been on Earth.

Though I have lived in few countries in Europe, in addition to the UK, I find Europe to be a very homely place. The European Union (EU) has been the best social, economic, and perhaps quasi-political institution in the world, doing so much to make life better for everyone in the world. The million nice things about the EU were evident on the morning of the Brexit vote when I saw work colleagues shedding tears as a result of the Brexit vote. I felt like I was somewhere in Africa attending a funeral; it was a good testimony to the bond that the EU has created with its people.

Asia is a fascinating continent and sometimes it can be confusing whether or not the Middle East is part of Asia. In Asia, I lived in Kabul, Afghanistan, for one year and eight months; Afghanistan borders mainland China to the east. On the day I was taking off from Dubai International Airport to Kabul International Airport in January 2006, I had some disappointing conversations with a passenger in the airport. It is normal for passengers to exchange information about their next destination while in the airport. I happened to talk to a person *en route* to the Middle East and he asked me where I was heading to. The mention of Afghanistan really rattled the passenger and he stopped short of saying please head to somewhere else that is less dangerous. It reminded me that two months earlier, I was happily working in Britain and had just taken a long vacation in Kenya before the expat job came knocking fast in my second week of a long planned holiday in Kenya. In fact, it was the visa that delayed me, otherwise I would have been in Afghanistan much earlier. But the fun of working in a multi-cultural environments where everyone matters is too tempting and always worth the price.

In Afghanistan, I really enjoyed the Asian life. The international organisation was a vibrant one with colleagues from India, Nepal, Bangladesh, European countries, African countries, the USA, Australia, and even Latin America. It was a global melting pot. My flight from Dubai to Kabul was interesting and we took a long route to Kabul; because of military intervention in Afghanistan, the flight path was a bit long and we approached Kabul from the north. There was deep snow in January and I had read about the winter in the Old Russia Territory.

The earth from the sky was full of snow and I wondered if the runway would be safe. In the quest for The Diaspora, our elder son was in Kenya with my mum and mum-in-law while my wife was an MBA student in the UK. Sometimes I wondered whether it was worth taking the risk. Around thirty minutes to landing, the pilot announced the start of descending to Kabul. It was a lovely flight, relatively calm with no normal shaking, though it was freezing snowy weather. I was somehow fascinated, perhaps alert due to historic aviation incidents in Kabul. Ten minutes to landing, the pilot made the usual announcement and soon we had reached densely snowy Kabul. The pilot went around Kabul, descending twice progressively, and as a first-timer it was a bit frightening and I thought maybe he was trying to figure out the runway, which I talked to myself, saying "it has to be somewhere". In few minutes, we made a sudden landing, perhaps landing like a bus as they call it. Funnily people cheered and clapped, it was a nice welcome to Kabul, the city surrounded by nice mountains.

I did not understand why the pilot made such a landing plan but I knew the pilot was experienced as he had grey hair and was almost balding. I later learnt that landing in Kabul must take at least a cycle or two over Kabul in a descending path because Kabul is circled by mountains which are very high on one side so direct descent and landing is impossible, however take-off must be one-sided as we know it. Kabul was very interesting and so was Afghanistan. It was fascinating, amazing. The food was very nice and we enjoyed the Friday barbeque, buffet, and free drinks provided by one of the best international organisations one would wish to work for. Lunchtime in Kabul was lovely with smell of lovely goat meat throughout the city and Afghan bread being ferried around and about.

I was always a security-conscious person, very covert at times, and I dealt with lots of money as head of finance, administration, and human resources. In the eighteen months I was there, no single penny was lost and the organisation grew very well, and I was saddened to leave Asia after twenty months to go back to England. I would love to go back to Asia; it is a fascinating place with good people and plenty of food.

Interestingly though, what kept me going was the excellent environment in Afghanistan. In the organisation, I had formed a bible study group of friends from the Philippines and West Africa, and we met every Sunday morning for prayers. It was a fascinating time getting the best out of Asia.

I still believe to date that while in Afghanistan, a miracle happened. I once woke up shaking badly, and God was talking to me about something, perhaps about my trip to Asia. To date, I still marvel about that encounter with God.

In Africa, I worked in Kenya before university, then in Hargeisa Somaliland, and most recently in South Sudan, the newest country in the world. My arrival to South Sudan was equally another strange journey. I had accepted the new job while working in the UK and the July 2016 conflict had started in South Sudan. News stories were frightening. I could see flight evacuations and all the bad news. I called a few people in Kenya, especially family and non-family members, and one of the non-family members said "Please mind your life first." My family is usually diplomatic, and some would speak in parables, for example to say "God will find you great opportunities". Well, I needed an opportunity then, and I had already signed a contract. Though I reserved the right to say no, I normally tend to be too diplomatic unless rattled or unsettled in a way, and perhaps the only time I act like a volcano, perhaps a strong attribute of being a member of The Diaspora, which is to know when to be diplomatic and when to rattle like an emergency aircraft on an urgent mission.

International adventure, excessive risk, daring moves, calculated and timed moves, have been very rewarding. I may not have held quickly financially enriching positions in life, but experience has been second to none, all financed cleverly. I must thank God the Almighty for keeping me in good health. Nothing is possible without good health. Of course, the experience may have taken some toll on health but anything can have an impact on human life and health. Even a rich king in a palace with all he needs for life does age and get into the traps of good lifestyle, and this informs why I am a religious person. I believe in liberty, democracy, rule of law, unlimited potential, freedom of choice, sovereignty of life, and sanctity of life. Love God whatever your religion is and love thy neighbour whoever that is, may appear as the old stories, but such simple beliefs would make our world a better place to live—this is my wish to the human race and The Diaspora.

Everyone has the good old stories of when life was simple and not complicated; when kids would play outside in mud and not with modern technology; when parents were the law and authority; the good old days could be the days the world badly needs.

International adventure has been interesting. I had the choice never to leave my homeland and work hard to be successful worker and businessman, and perhaps grow very rich but with limited knowledge. I chose another path initially called The Diaspora and subsequently the path in The Diaspora has been endless, one leading to another one as if contagious. One journey leading to another with almost no effort, but competitively obtained.

Many times I have applied for jobs in global websites with many making the same applications. God has helped me to succeed and I do not remember letting down my employers. This compelled me to write this personal history in dedication to my children and kids and many people around the world aspiring for self-determination. Walking the journey, defying all odds, making difficult decisions, taking risks, and most importantly, believing in God.

In my adventure in The Diaspora I was literally my own advisor with inputs from my wife. I had no tangible story to read about The Diaspora since most people do not reveal their ways and paths. When I headed to The Diaspora, especially the USA, information was very limited. Social media was not active then like it is now. Information was only available from marketing departments of major universities, one of which

125

made a great presentation in Nairobi and I signed right away to head to the free world, the United States. I hope you find this book useful and will assist The Diaspora globally.

A special dedication to the lovely countries in **Slide 5** below who made my journey in The Diaspora great, much better than I could ask for.

Slide 5 - No nation should be left behind: All nations matter. Education should be a game changer
by Hillary Rono @ Life in The Diaspora – countries of adventure from 12 hrs position then clockwise

The Diaspora in future

The Diaspora is here to stay and has been successful right from the ancient times. The Diaspora prompts one to think outside the comfort zone and outside the box. Countries that have refused to welcome The Diaspora have lagged behind economically compared to the ones that have supported The Diaspora.

The Diaspora that emanate from peaceful conditions succeed much like The Diaspora forced outside their homelands. Jews remain the most successful people the world has ever known in The Diaspora. Despite persecution over the years, Jews survived and thrived around the world until the establishment of the modern State of Israel in 1948. Global measures of economy have always put Israel in the top 35 out of 191 countries on Earth, despite being one of the smallest countries on Earth. Israel as we know it is a land of The Diaspora since it was re-established.

The Diaspora of Indian origin has been quite successful outside the original country of India and have succeeded in The Diaspora in Africa, Europe, and America more so in business and in science. Today, Indian pharmaceutical companies supply medication and drugs to a lot of countries around the world.

After the overthrow of Siad Barre of Somalia in 1991, political instability and anarchy led most Somalis to flee their homeland to neighbouring countries, especially Kenya, and into far lands, especially the West. The Somalis in The Diaspora has been a living testimony of the power of The

Diaspora. When I worked in Somaliland in 1991–2001, Somalis had massive queues in Dahabshil, a money exchange bureau, to receive billions of dollars from The Diaspora family members around the world. The queues never reduced each day for the whole month and I found them even busier than banks in the capital Nairobi.

The Diaspora remains the most important and powerful constituent of any nation. Its influence cuts across the entire society and touches social, economic, and political dimensions. The most felt impact of The Diaspora is usually economic, social, and then political.

Economic impact ranks high in impact since this normally remains the priority of any member of The Diaspora. Social impact is usually lagging since social impact requires physical presence and The Diaspora spend the least time in their original country. But The Diaspora continues to make a social impact, especially on social media. The political impact of The Diaspora has been felt the least because political impact requires The Diaspora members themselves to engage in politics by being physically present, a requirement that makes it hard for The Diaspora to engage in both worlds, that is, the native and newly adopted country.

Even though many countries have embraced and accepted dual nationality, many countries still fear having dual nationals actively participate in governance in their original countries because of a fear of meddling in their politics. This fear is usually out of unfounded sovereignty concerns.

In most countries, children of self-exiled members of The Diaspora retain the right to the nationality of their parents. Most children in The Diaspora get their parents' citizenship automatically, despite being born abroad. The children of The Diaspora remain untapped and perhaps not so well-known. Progressive governments ought to tap into this resource by establishing ways to engage with such constituents—the world remains dynamic, with lots of ideas, and deliberate government actions to engage with such constituents could emerge in the future especially a way of boosting bilateral ties through cultural means.

At the family level in The Diaspora, we hope for continuous efforts by The Diaspora community to engage the children of The Diaspora with those of cousins back in their homelands in an effort to forge enduring special relationships that are above the spatial and temporal divide.

As aforementioned, The Diaspora started because of a range of factors, mainly economic and political. The big question in future for any government is the ability to monitor The Diaspora movements and capitalise on the trends. In some emerging economies, the conditions that made The Diaspora move outside their homelands may have changed favourably—it could be growing economy or political maturity—but the big question remains whether The Diaspora will opt to return to their homelands.

Returning back to the homeland remains a very difficult decision for any member of The Diaspora and it remains to be seen what The Diaspora will do in future. However, due to the complexities of life, it is doubtful whether any large group of The Diaspora will all make the same decision, leading to mass migration of people. Furthermore, it may not be very easy for countries of origin to start initiatives that will pull The Diaspora in large numbers.

The UK has in the past tried to statistically measure immigration and emigration trends, but it is very complicated and controversial and it created a political storm between labour and the conservatives. In fact, the planned departure by the UK from the European Union resulted in the Brexit vote, which in itself was the result of a heated debate on immigration. The UK, one of the most successful empires the world has ever known, remains dogged in the process of exiting the EU. In fact, what unsettled hard-line Brexiteers was the fact that EU laws take precedence over UK laws, especially those touching on human rights. This means if the EU law unsettled UK law it would have been largely due to immigration, itself driven by The Diaspora, and in the UK context, The Diaspora would be global citizens settling down in the UK.

The fact is that governments will continue to bicker about immigration, but really what drives immigration are a complex set of factors that can extend beyond the boundaries of a sovereign country. Before the collapse of Somalia in 1991, very few people in the neighbouring countries, especially Kenya, would ever have imagined having to host Somali nationals and refugees, but the changes, a mix of positive and negative, happened slowly, sometimes not being so noticeable until they were too big for the host government of Kenya. Similarly, UK immigration and the resulting large number of The Diaspora from countries around the world was a slow and permanent shift caused by a complex set of factors; politicians may deny this, bicker about it, or do whatever they deem best, but trends will keep changing until they are too powerful for action – who knew one day frustrated immigrants would literary walk to continental Europe after the Syria crisis.

Migration is too powerful for any single country to handle and the Syria crisis was a big reminder of the reasons why migration can be a divine move beyond human understanding. The Jewish migration globally lasted for a long time, and Jews went to nearly every country on Earth and finally returned to Israel.

For any scholar of geography, particularly with a focus on migration of people, the Brexit vote would not have been a surprise. It was shocking how everyone reacted following the surprise vote. What many people forget is to take a step back and reflect hard. The UK has been one of the most successful countries internationally. Indeed, the Commonwealth of Nations was founded after the UK gave control of many foreign territories it had occupied. What is often forgotten is the impact that global movement of the UK would later have in the UK.

For the UK to succeed, most of its nationals needed to work abroad in The Diaspora and over the years, UK nationals have been quite successful in The Diaspora, perhaps among the most sought after due to a mix of high quality values. The success of members of The Diaspora originally from UK meant a strong economy for the UK, which leads to more jobs in the UK mainland. Unfortunately, UK population growth has over the years failed to keep pace with economic growth, economic expansion, and massive foreign investments in the UK.

For many years, the UK faced skill shortages that would only be filled by foreign workers. For any observer or statistician during the boom years in the UK, it was very clear that in few years' time, the foreign workforce would increase significantly in the UK, and as we know it, controlling people is a very difficult task.

131

The global crisis in 2008 did not affect the UK much. However, the fears of job losses gave way to immigration questions. Immigration was already complicated by EU law and pro-Brexiteers found a way to sell the Brexit narrative. The scope of this book is The Diaspora and to sum it up, The Diaspora in the UK, either abroad or in mainland, has led to a new term in the world that is emerging, namely "the Brexit". The impact of Brexit is something to watch, and The Diaspora in the UK and around the world continue to monitor it as it is bound to have a huge impact.

But The Diaspora will survive the Brexit example and move on into the future. But there will be a lot of lessons learnt.

Conclusion

The Diaspora is a journey and involves a lot of processes. It is complicated but can be fun. One risks everything but gets better bargains. Earlier, I described causes of immigration and thus The Diaspora as economic, political, and social. Advanced nations welcomed political immigrants escaping trouble and also welcomed economic migrants who added value to the national prosperity but restricted social migrants, especially those accompanying earlier political and economic migrants.

Heading into the unknown is never easy. When people moved to The Diaspora in the past there was not so much information about the destination until information technology informed us lots, especially after the year 2000. Social media has said it all about The Diaspora, which is good, as people get well-informed before taking big steps.

No two journeys into The Diaspora will be alike. One will have a different encounter. But what matters is the end result, and everyone's wish is a good end in a world of endless red tape and barriers. But the basic tips of life can see one through the long journey in The Diaspora.

I hope this book, based on real life experience in The Diaspora across many countries (especially those in blue in **Slide 6** below), shed some light about The Diaspora and helps to make informed decision. Good luck in your journey in The Diaspora.

Slide 6 - Every nation matter: The greatest lesson learnt in The Diaspora is <u>play by the rules</u>
by Hillary Rono @ Life in The Diaspora

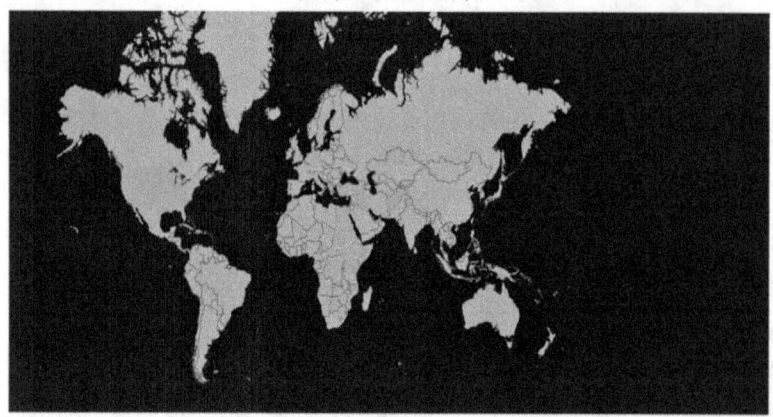

The Author

In September 1999, Hillary Rono got his first job in The Diaspora even before he sat his final paper at the University of Nairobi, Kenya. Since then, Hillary has lived in six countries outside his country of birth in Kenya, and the stay in four of the six countries ranges from twenty months to twelve years each. Originally, Hillary never wanted to leave his country of birth, Kenya. What started as educational migration turned into economic migration, followed by settlement in a new country, miles away from his country of origin; it is an extraordinary journey.

For aspiring immigrants, this provides a good guide about moving abroad. As a minimum, it provides some certainty into the unknown world and some basic facts to start off with.

Hillary managed to stay legally in all countries and strongly advocates for legal migration. Hillary faced immigration challenges like any other immigrant but personally and diligently dealt with all of them on his own, with technical advice when necessary.

While still an immigrant, Hillary advised lots of immigrants trying to sort out their immigration issues with cases ranging from simple to complex ones. Motivated by hands-on experience in immigration, Hillary is commencing a course to convert his academic and professional qualifications into a Graduate Diploma in Law (GDL) with the University of Law in the UK, in January 2018.

Hillary has over fifteen years' experience working with some of the most successful international non-governmental organisations (INGOs), with some commercial experience, all gained in four continents of the world.

Hillary is married with three boys and lives in England, and frequently visits his original homeland of Kenya. This is Hillary's first book and more will be on the way, just to share life experiences which matter to people, hoping readers will gain some life skills based on true stories. Indeed, there is no better teacher in life than hands-on experience and on immigration issues, it provides a one stop shop to learn the often ignored basics that matter so much, and form the bedrock of big things and big decisions.

The second book by Hillary, will be about distance learning with the title "The Successful Distance Learning Adventure" and will provide useful tips to people around the world thinking about distance learning. It will describe in a brief book, a hands on approach to distance learning which can be used by virtually everyone, every household on earth, in the quest for education just like the quest for The Diaspora.

Thank you.

www.ingramcontent.com/pod-product-compliance
Lightning Source LLC
Chambersburg PA
CBHW060357290526
45791CB00002B/539